"You're Not My Mommy!" WARNINGS from an Ex-Stepmother

Donna Jarrett

Copyright © 2013 Donna Jarrett

All rights reserved.

ISBN: 978-0-9897658-1-7

For my brother Mark

CONTENTS

Acknowledgments

Introduction 1

1 He Had Me At Hello: 3
A Gentle Introduction to Stepmotherdom

2 This is a Warning: 11
Listen to the Dings before you put on that Ring!

3 When Things Get Real: 24
Challenges and Changes as a Full Time Momma

4 No Romance without Finance: 38
Babies, Budgets and Bank Balances

5 The Emotional Rollercoaster: 50
Guarding Your Heart in the Ups and Downs of Love

6 The Case of the Ex: 60
How to Avoid Baby-mama Drama

7 Faith and Love: 70
The Role of Religion in your Relationship

8 When Two Become One: 75
Saying Goodbye to the Child That isn't Yours

9 You, Me and Baby Makes Three: 84
Motherhood vs. Stepmotherhood

10 You're Not My Mommy! You're Not My Wife: 94
The Curious Case of the Stepgirlfriend

11 All's Well That Ends Well: 105
Life After Stepmotherhood

ACKNOWLEDGMENTS

I am deeply grateful to my mother, Judy Jarrett, who worked hard every day but came home to ensure we were educated, fed, clothed and cleaned. I learned a lot from you. Thank you so much for being a good mother.

To my step-father, James Young, who loved me as his own, helping to create a wonderful environment for us all as a child.

To Lachelle, my best friend of over twenty years. Thank you for being my sounding board.

To my sisters, Chicana and Desta who have helped me to understand what sacrifice means in motherhood.

To my brother James, a living example of what it means to be a great dad. To my late, great brother Mark, who protected me and was the funniest man alive, rest in peace.

To Joanne Griffith, what can I say? I would not have been able to produce this wonderful project without you. Ready for more my friend?

To Kate Maruyama, the greatest editor I know. Thank you for being prompt and concise.

To my traveling buddies and friends at work, thank you for your positive energy and optimism in helping to celebrate this book.

To my husband Drew: My stallion, optimistic critic, sounding board and personal bartender for those late nights of reading and wonderful conversations. You are the true meaning of a man.

INTRODUCTION

Of all the things in the world that I have wanted to do, writing a book was not one of them. Yet, here it is, a brief beat of my life laid bare on these pages. Why? Because I had to.

Being a stepmother is one of the toughest, most thankless, emotionally draining tasks that you will take on as a woman. It's also a role stuffed to the brim with the greatest joys you will ever experience. But no one talks about it. It's as though in becoming a stepmom you join a secret sorority vowed to silence because ordinary women can't handle the truth. Well, I've been there and while the reality of being a stepmom is far from sunshine and roses every day, being prepared is the key to maintaining your sanity while performing a balancing act of epic proportions on the high wire of life.

When I started on my stepmotherhood journey, I was like a carpenter trying to build an elaborate cabinet with only children's toys for tools. Have you ever tried to turn a screw with a piece of plastic? You can only finish even the simplest of tasks with the right equipment.

There is an abundance of books, magazines, blogs and online forums on what to expect through pregnancy and motherhood, but there's very little for stepmothers. You won't see free magazines and handouts on being a stepmom at your OB/GYN, that's for sure. Yet the role of "stepping in for Mom" is far more complex, challenging and fraught with problems that you just don't see coming. You need the right tools to handle this!

"You're Not My Mommy!" WARNINGS from an Ex-Stepmother

Over the years I have spoken with countless women who have shared their stepmothering horror story. I knew what I wanted to tell them - "run for the hills, girl!" - but I didn't. It wasn't what many of them wanted to hear, and I didn't want to be the one to burst their bubble.

Now, with a decade of personal experience as a stepmother and wife to a man who struggled to provide for his own family, I have to speak the truth. I'm still not saying, "Run, friend, RUN!" but you need to know what you're getting into. If you've just started a relationship with a man with children, read and digest every page: you will encounter every issue highlighted and so much more. If you're already a stepmom and you need some tools to get you through those challenging moments, find the chapter that speaks to what you're going through now and refer back whenever you need to.

Children aren't a burden, they're a blessing and I thank God every day for the three lights he brought into my life when I married my now ex-husband. They taught me so much and made me a better person and for that I'm thankful. The drama with their daddy? We'll get into that.

This book is for you. A resource, a roadmap, a cheaper-than-therapy guide to navigating the land of stepmotherhood. When you reach a roadblock in your journey, open these pages and know that you're part of an international sisterhood that shares your every pain, every reason to laugh and the frustration behind every teardrop.

You are not alone.

CHAPTER ONE

He Had Me at Hello:
A Gentle Introduction to Stepmotherdom

His eyes peeked like a sunrise over the horizon of a new day as he handed me flowers in full bloom. Quick as a flash, he hurried away, masking his brilliant smile, but there was no way he could hide his cuteness. I followed his gaze until it was out of sight and right there on the sidewalk outside my job in Midtown Manhattan, I fell in love. Never mind that the guy in question was barely three feet tall and preferred to bury his head in the safety of his father's knees. I loved this little guy from hello.

It was the first meeting with my then boyfriend's two year old son, just months into our relationship. I thought my heart would melt. It was the first of many fun times with my boyfriend, his son - who I called Little Man - and me. It was also the first of many get togethers with my boyfriend's three children. Yes, I said three. Did you hear that record scratch? I didn't realize it at the time, but the GPS to my life was rerouting. Next stop? Destination Stepmommaville.

It's a strange place, stepmotherhood. In one breath you're adored, but alienated. Part of the family, yet a stranger. An authority figure, but completely powerless. You live your life in a space between worlds where your tools of survival combine the patience of Mother Teresa, a Teflon-coated skin to deal with the guaranteed hurtful words coming your way, and the diplomacy skills of Kofi Annan. It's a lot.

"You're Not My Mommy!" WARNINGS from an Ex-Stepmother

Truthfully, I had no clue what I was letting myself in for. If I had, I would have backed up out of there leaving nothing but dust and tire marks behind. But I was in l-o-v-e. It's hard to foresee baby-mama drama, financial ruin and emotional bankruptcy through the haze of rose-tinted glasses. Yet life put me on this particular journey for a reason – for better, for worse and for better again.

My pathway to stepparenthood starts in 2001, a year forever linked to the unforgettable atrocity of the September 11th terrorist attacks on the World Trade Center in New York. Sadly, 2001 was already bad for me, long before those planes smashed into the Twin Towers.

Scroll back to March 2001 and a family games night in Long Island. We were all gathered at my parents' house, ready to eat food and throw down on the games front. Only one person was missing: my brother, Mark. We called and verbally tussled with him, telling him to hurry up so we could start. He laughed and said he was on his way. Mark never came. Instead, the door my brother was meant to walk through was filled with police officers telling us he was gone.

Our sibling, my parents' son, killed by a car as he crossed a street. I ran out of the house, refusing to believe that my brother was dead. Dead? How could that be? We had just spoken! I raced into my car and towards the scene of the accident, believing the officers had it all wrong and they'd made a terrible mistake. But they were right. I watched as my brother's once vibrant, now lifeless body was hauled into the coroner's van and the doors closed with deafening finality on a life taken too soon. That image of my brother Mark is stained on my memory.

"You're Not My Mommy!" WARNINGS from an Ex-Stepmother

I tried to keep my mind and my body in motion. Between informing family and friends of Mark's death, helping to plan the funeral and taking care of my brother's affairs, my grieving process was slow and at times solitary.

As the days after my brother's passing turned into weeks and months, I slowly started to heal and a friend invited me to the Bronx where she was selling vintage clothing. I love the hustle and bustle of New York, with people talking, spontaneous laughter and heated conversation, all merging to bounce energy off the sidewalks and wrap anyone in close proximity with healing vibes, if only for a moment.

While we were there, my friend introduced me to a sweet looking guy, full of wide smiles and a warming spirit. I caught myself thinking. "Hmmm...maybe." My brother's death changed me, made me vulnerable and brought to the surface my need to be loved, to be held and to not have to go through all of this hurt and pain alone. But as quickly as the thought appeared it was gone – and so was the smiley guy.

Months after our first encounter, I was in a beauty salon when in he walked, the guy with the smile, selling some of his beautiful jewelry. I purchased a ring I liked and Smiley Guy came over, all Luther Vandross; "Excuse me miss, what's your name? Where are you from? Can I call? Or possibly, can I take you out tonight?" What followed were many phone calls and conversations. There was that indescribable "something."

At the time, The Potential was living in Atlanta with his mother. Geez – red flag, much? But a girl's got a heart and needs, so I ignored the warning sign that said "Has three children who don't live with him and *he* lives with his mama. HELLO?!!!" My instinct lost its voice from shouting at me to walk away from this guy, but I wanted to see if the connection we felt down the telephone line was just as real in person. Well I guess the answer was yes. Shortly after my trip to Atlanta, The Potential was upgraded to The Boyfriend and I put him in my pocket and took him home.

Why, oh why, oh why did I do that? It doesn't take a rocket scientist to conclude that our relationship was doomed from the start. We were very different people - I had an established career in finance, along with all of the trappings of that world, such as vacations and a comfortable home. The Boyfriend on the other hand, was a hustler. He owned a vending business selling handmade jewelry mainly in New York, but he would also travel to lucrative festivals for weeks at a time. Sounds glamorous, but his income barely scratched the surface of his outgoings, let alone our household expenses. Talk about Mars and Venus

So why were we together? Life circumstances. The loss of both our brothers in 2001, plus the heartache of September 11, 2001 made me not want to be alone to suffer through these hardships. In hindsight, anyone could have come along at that time and I would probably have felt the same way. I was crowded by emotion, and he was my escape.

All this said, I must give The Boyfriend some credit. He was honest with me about his life and all of its trials and tribulations and the hopes he had for his children. I just chose to ignore him. My bad.

March 11th, 2006: The Bahamas. Another relationship

upgrade – this time from The Boyfriend to The Husband. Under the tropical sun, we joined in holy matrimony surrounded by seventy of our nearest and dearest. Sadly, none of The Husband's children could be there. The problem? Finance. Or lack thereof. Another day, another warning, but I missed it. Too much water in my ears from whipping through the cool Caribbean water on a jet ski!

A year later, with our feet on dry land, circumstances brought The Husband's son, Little Man, in to our home full-time. Put plainly, his mother threw him out on the street in the middle of the night and then called to tell us to collect him. Forget instant coffee, this was instant motherhood. Just take my life and add a child.

Even though the introduction to a 24/7 life together was unconventional, there was nothing I wouldn't do for Little Man. I turned my home life, my finances and my heart upside down. Moved from a condo in Queens to a house with a yard on Long Island.

Added Little Man to my benefits, found him a great school. But when it came to Mother's Day, he only had eyes for his mama. It hurt. A lot.

And that's why I'm writing this. Not to pour scorn and complain about life as a stepmother, but to expose the realities of stepping into a ready-made family. When you marry a man with children, you will forever have another woman in your life: his ex. You will be viewed with a level of suspicion by his children, maybe for awhile, maybe always. Your finances will become exposed; you will be vulnerable to a level of drama that your single self would never tolerate.

You will give your heart to someone who is not your blood relative, and, if your marriage doesn't work out, your rights to the relationship you've cultivated with your children from another mother will be non-existent. And you won't even have a hand painted card with your name on it to show for all your effort.

Don't think it won't happen to you. The thing is, if you're of an age to be in a relationship, you may well end up being a stepparent. In the United States, 50 percent of first marriages end in divorce. 60 percent of second time nuptials also wind up in Splitsville. So it's no surprise that 14 percent of women in the United States are stepmothers to children under 18. And just one more statistic for you - according to the Census Bureau, 42 percent of adults in the United States will experience some kind of step relationship, either as the parent, or the child. So in short, it's all around us and you could be next.

Would you start a new job without researching the company? Would you go on vacation without checking out the resort? Would you bake a cake you've never attempted before without a recipe? Probably no to all of the above. So why would you consider becoming a stepmother without thinking about what you're getting yourself into? Take it from me as a woman who's swum in the waters of stepmotherhood, this is a decision you can't make based solely on being in love. You need real life, straight, no chaser advice and that's where my life and my experience come in.

I wish I once had someone to talk to about being a stepmother. I didn't and that's why I've committed my thoughts to the page, to try to help. But be warned, this advice is not for the faint-hearted!

I'm not bashing men with children. Nor am I saying that all stepmother/stepchild relationships will be torturous and difficult. But it's important to understand that being a stepmother isn't for everyone. If you do decide to go ahead or you're already living life as a stepmother, this book will steer you through some key questions that you should ask yourself, as you navigate one of the toughest family dynamics around:

- *What impact will being with a man with children have on your personal finances?*

- *What changes will you have to make to your lifestyle to accommodate a ready-made family?*

- *If you want children, does your partner want to have more?*

- *How is your partner making provisions for his family without drawing on your resources?*

- *What is his relationship with his ex and what contact are you expected to have with her?*

- *How is your emotional state? How will you cope with the mother always being number one, even when the children live with you?*

- *What rights do you have as a stepmother or stepgirlfriend?*

- *What are the warning signs you need to look out for that may let you know this isn't the relationship for you?*

Throughout these pages, I'll share my personal experience

from those first heady days of love to the painful end of my marriage and help you decide whether you want to step into this relationship, or step right off.

CHAPTER TWO

This is a Warning:
Listen to the Dings before you put on that Ring!

Instinct is a good thing: that tingle, that gut reaction, those hairs on the back of your neck when something just isn't *quite* right. The feeling can be affirming or alarming, but just as animals are the first to run for cover when a storm is on the way, that physical reaction is the manifestation of an external action

When it came to The Husband, my own early warning system was off the charts, alerting me to the tsunami of trouble that was about to wash over and potentially wipe out my life. But I did nothing. I was a lame duck waiting for someone to shout, "Incoming!"

There were reasons, of course. I was happy and in love, content to get wrapped up in the many good moments we shared. We laughed a lot, our physical chemistry was great, we had a busy social life. My stepchildren were not a presence in our lives on a daily basis, but a very welcome addition. In many ways, I was a stepmother on the sidelines, always happy to see them, but with no real influence or say in how they were raised. In time that would change, but for a large portion of our life together, The Husband and I enjoyed the best of both worlds: the positive energy that little people can bring into your life, but without the sleepless nights, kiddie drama, financial burden and day to day mess they can create.

Still, there were things that troubled me about The Husband, including his actions and general attitude towards me even before we tied the knot. Here's an example: I'm a neat-freak. I like my home to be kept just so and everyone who knows me knows that.

One day I left The Husband at home with his children and went to work. When I walked back through the door twelve hours later, my condo was in such a mess I thought someone had broken in. There was food and dirty dishes, clothes, paper all over the place. Needless to say, I didn't hide my displeasure. The Husband looked sheepish and cleaned up, but why did he let the place get that way knowing that such untidiness in my home is a big no-no? No respect, that's why.

But that was the day I also learned The Husband was driving around town in my car with another woman. That really got me hot under the collar. Especially when it turned out to be his baby-mama. I was not okay with this. First of all, how did he even begin to think it was ok for him to give his ex a ride in my car when she'd made it clear she didn't like me? And second, what a way to confuse the children! Can you imagine the dialog in their minds? "Why is Daddy in Donna's car with Mommy?" The Husband didn't stop to think beyond what was most convenient for him. He didn't consider me and he didn't consider his children.

Just these two examples should have been enough to give me pause. With each passing day I had more questions that neither his actions nor his mouth could adequately answer. But I don't blame him. If I'd asked the right questions before getting married, The Husband would never have had a chance to put a ring on it. Maybe I knew that and was scared of what would happen.

But ladies, let me tell you this. If there are issues relating to your husband or partner and your relationship with his children, don't expect them to miraculously disappear without you staging an intervention. Issues left unchallenged simply magnify and multiply like germs in a Petri dish. I tried so hard to silence my inner voice and I have paid dearly in time, money and a little piece of my trusting soul.

My own mother said something very telling at my bridal shower, just weeks before I walked down the aisle. "Always make sure you stay true to yourself. If you don't feel good about something, bail out." It was odd hearing that from her. She had no axe to grind as far as being a stepparent was concerned; she herself had remarried and my stepfather was a good guy. But her words didn't sit right with me. Why? Because my instinct was ringing the alarm. "Abandon ship!" Oh, I'm just so stubborn...

Of course every relationship has its own creases to straighten out, but if you are entering a partnership where children are involved, there are certain alarm bells you should listen for and deal with accordingly. Now, I'm not saying you should leave: that is your choice. But as with everything, you should go in with your eyes wide open. And be ready to cast yourself a lifeline should you need it.

ALARM ONE: "I can't live alone"

Ray Parker Jr. once said that man should not sleep alone. Ok, that's fine, I mean, who really wants to sleep alone on a regular basis? But a man who tells you he *can't* live alone, or has never lived a solo life? Your feet should be stuffed into your sneakers and heading for the front door leaving Usain Bolt standing in your dust.

When we first met, The Husband was living with his mother in Atlanta while his ex took care of their three children in New York. I remember asking him one day, "Why don't you get your own place?" thinking that it would make it easier for his children to visit and give them a place to stay, should they ever need it. He responded that he just didn't like living alone. "I like to have people around at all times," he said. I blinked in disbelief, my brain unable to compute that a grown man was telling me he would prefer to live with his mama than by himself, even as the father of three young children. Hmmm...

This lack of desire to live alone, especially for men with children, can speak to:

- *A lack of responsibility.*

Running a home means paying bills, learning to budget on one salary and taking care of necessities such as grocery shopping, cooking and laundry. Never lived alone? Then you've never exercised this muscle, and if you have children, how can you be an example to them? Answer: You can't.

- *A lack of foresight.*

If your partner shares parenting with another person, there could come a day when the children are in his care full-time, for any number of reasons. If he doesn't have a place of his own to call home, where will his children stay? Even if this is a situation that looks highly unlikely today, as the old Boy Scout motto says: "Always be prepared."

- *A lack of maturity.*

There comes a time when all adults should crave their own space. Found a guy who doesn't want to live alone? You may soon become more of a mother figure to him than an object of desire.

Now, I'm not including men who live with a roommate in this

equation, providing there are no children in his life. If he has kids, he has responsibilities and this means he needs to put their current and future needs first.

This leads to the second warning:

ALARM TWO: "Honey, my money is funny"

Everything in life doesn't have a dollar amount attached. It's true; the best things in life are free. But love doesn't pay the rent, pay for clothes, purchase school supplies or put food on the table. Back in the real world, cold hard cash is king.

The Husband was financially unstable for the bulk of our relationship. He made his living as a glorified salesman selling handcrafted jewelry at festivals, fairs and by dropping into local stores. This was fine when he was a single man, but as a father, this working style didn't provide a reliable income or any company benefits.

On top of this, The Husband had no credit of any kind. In many ways, he was a walking John Doe, flying under the radar of adult life. There was no doubt that The Husband loved his kids: he was there to listen to them, to laugh, to have fun and let them know they were loved. But some of the financial brass tacks of raising a child were missing and left his children vulnerable.

As a woman stepping into this kind of situation, there are some potential problems you may face:

- *His lack of money will impact your shared household finances.*

A man with no job is one who can't support himself, let alone you. If you live with him, kiss a chunk of your check goodbye. You'll be using it to keep the house afloat and the wolf from your door. Say bye bye to your mani/pedi.

- *You could be expected to spring for days out.*

If you're out as a family and the children know their dad is low on funds, they may look to you, all doe-eyed and cute and ask for an ice cream and soda. Not that you should mind doing this, but small things can soon become big expectations on all sides.

Here's an example:

A year into our marriage, one of my stepchildren came to live with us. It was unexpected, and our home at the time, while spacious, was still a one bedroom duplex which wasn't suitable for two adults and a young boy. Before long, we were looking at four bedroom homes in Long Island to accommodate our new family situation, but this cost money. The Husband had none, so I pulled funds from my condo to use as a down payment. I was doing it for our family, to give the child a place to stay and to grow. Now, that the marriage is over, I'm left with the payments, the debt and a headache.

- *You may have to add the children to your company benefits.*

If you have a stable job and are with a man who doesn't, if one or all of the children come to live with you full-time, it may seem only responsible to include them on your company benefits. Oh yes, this will cost. Again, this is part of being a parent, but it will hit your financial bottom line if the father is not in a position to contribute.

- *Your partner is paying child support.*

Every man should pay what he owes to raise his kids. However, as the new woman stepping in, his check may only go so far and, as such, may curtail some of the things the two of you would like to do financially as a couple, such as buy a home, take vacations or possibly have more children.

Yes, more children. Would you like your own? Funky finances may lead to a restrictive situation where your partner or husband is reluctant to bring another mouth to feed into this world. This could lead to animosity over your own desires to be a mother and his feeling that he's contributed enough to the continuation of the human race. You have to know if this is a deal breaker for you.

ALARM THREE: Babies, Toddlers, Grown Children

This is a touchy subject and dependent on the individual. When I first met The Husband, his children were aged three, two and one.

Being so close in age actually wasn't the problem. The fact they were so young when we met, especially the last child who was barely able to walk and talk at a year old, was a huge issue and a big alarm. For me, it spoke to The Husband's character. Are you really going to start a new relationship when you have so recently gone through a momentous life-changing act with the mother of your children? How could things turn so sour in less than a year? How can you turn your back on this woman and not only walk away, but start a new life with another woman? It made me question his integrity as a man, his resolve as a father and whether he had the staying power to go the distance in a relationship when the going got tough.

Things happen and relationships aren't so cut and dried. You can find yourself in a situation where you love the child that you made, but you just know in your heart that you won't be sharing a lifetime of memories with your baby's mama or daddy. I get it, but I couldn't help but ask myself "Would he be so quick to do the same thing to me?" Hmmm…

ALARM FOUR: A question of paternity

For the record, I have never been on Jerry Springer or appeared on an edition of Maury, or any other daytime "chat" show discussing DNA and paternity. However, the reality of today is that when some babies are born, folks start to ask, "Who's the Daddy?"

While reality TV offers free DNA testing in exchange for the rights to air all your dirty linen in public, the people, their stories and their feelings are real. Unless your life plays out like a soap opera, if your partner is either questioning or shares his doubts about a child he is fathering from a previous relationship, this needs to be addressed because:

- He may treat that child differently, potentially making it difficult for you to build a loving and sustainable relationship with the kid.

- He may be making a financial contribution to a child that isn't his. This sounds harsh, but being responsible for a child that doesn't share his DNA could place a monetary burden on your household and relationship.

- There's a statute of limitations when it comes to conducting DNA testing. If your partner is supporting a child he suspects is not his, start things off on the right foot and encourage him to get the paternity issue settled at the outset.

Once any man is on the hook for child support, it may very well be too late to turn back the clock. If at some point down the road evidence surfaces that a child may not be his, good luck trying to get your state's district attorney to agree to a DNA test at that point. It just ain't going to happen, folks.

- A child deserves to know who his real father is. Plain and simple. You never want them to find out with someone saying, "You know that's not your Daddy, right?" Where there's doubt, make sure you find out.

ALARM FIVE: The Ex doesn't realize it's over

This should be simple, but sometimes, what people *think* they have communicated, isn't necessarily *heard* by the receiving party. Let me explain.

I will always have a special place in my heart for the Bahamas. Not only is it warm when New York is in the pit of winter, but it's where The Husband proposed and where we later exchanged our wedding vows. At the time we were in a good place. He was working a regular job and handling his business.

So I was beyond blown away when The Husband asked for my hand in marriage as we played on jet skis. It was one of the most memorable and romantic moments of my life. Of course I said yes.

When we got home, we told the children about the engagement and they were happy and excited, asking to see the ring and oohing and ahhing at the sight of it.

The children in turn shared the news with their mother who had no interest in wishing us the best for our upcoming marriage. In fact, she was mad.

You see, she was still wearing the engagement ring The Husband had given to her many years before. She was also still wearing it on her wedding finger. Ouch. Even though they had not been together for a number of years, she had that one thing that will keep a woman hanging on: Hope.

I couldn't really blame her. At key moments, she was still treated like The Husband's significant other by his family. When his brother died, I offered to support him at the funeral, having lost my own brother just months before. I understood the fog of sadness he was feeling and wanted to be there for him. But there was no room for me, either physically or emotionally. The Ex occupied that space.

Closure is key in order for all parties involved to move on. In The Husband's case, it was unclear why they had broken up and his ex clearly didn't receive the memo. In her eyes they never formally parted, he simply got up and left. In his mind, that act ended their union. In The Ex's mind, his absence was simply a break in regular transmission.

Why is this an alarm? A woman scorned is not a woman you want in your life, even from a distance, and certainly not if you are spending time with her children and her ex-man. In addition, the chasm between The Husband's version of the break up and that of his Ex speaks to issues surrounding communication and being mindful of the feelings of others. Honestly, I understand her anger. Her feelings were hurt. And hurt people turn around and hurt other people.

ALARM SIX: When you don't seek the advice of others

Your own actions or lack of action should raise a red flag too.

Remember I told you about my mother's advice to always be true to myself? On more than one occasion she acted as a mirror for my soul, asking me questions and making statements that I had long ignored. "Why doesn't he [The Husband] work a regular job?" I couldn't (or wouldn't) answer that. "I really thought the two of you would have broken up by now." Oh yes, that. I honestly agreed with her, but always pushed the thought to the back of my mind. He really was a great guy and I really cared deeply for him. We really were in love.

But there were problems left unaddressed. Today, I can only blame myself for that. I have friends who are stepmothers, who would have issued real life warnings of what it means to be with a man with children. Embarrassment stopped me from reaching out. That, and the fact that I truly believed our love could conquer all. Yes, I know...

ALARM SEVEN: When your husband won't set boundaries with the children

Children have the ability, unintentionally, to make you feel really bad. You know how those tiny paper cuts can hurt the most? Children can have the same effect.

One of the highest hurdles you may have to jump as a stepmother is what you will be called. You're not "Mommy," but you have a significant place in your stepchildren's lives as the partner of their father. Or you should. That lack of title can leave you feeling insignificant on certain days. Room for a Stepmother's Day, anyone?

One day, The Husband came to collect me from work. Little Man was sitting in the back with a beautiful hand painted card peeping out the top of his bag. Forgetting myself, I asked him who the card was for. "My mommy" he said. "When I get home I'm going to pick a flower and give it to her with the card." I felt crushed, but couldn't show my emotions, after all, this wasn't about me. Little Man had made a beautiful gift for his mother, as he should have.

However, it made me realize that I would only ever be "Donna". The children called me by my first name, and it didn't sit right with me. That said, I didn't want to make a big deal of it as I still call my stepfather by his first name.

The Husband had never set out any ground rules for how the children should address me. A friend, who's also a stepmom, said her husband's children call her "Mom". Even the partners of my husband's brothers were given special names by their stepchildren.

The Husband saw no issue with me being called "Donna" by his children. Even though I enjoyed a good relationship with the kids, that small act of calling me by my name meant I lacked a level of authority in their lives.

Essentially, it put me on a par with them and in many ways invalidated my position in the family: it offered no permanence and I could be ejected out of their lives at anytime, as though I'd never been there.

ALARM EIGHT: When your husband won't set boundaries with other people

When you get involved with any man, regardless of whether he has children or not, you're also getting involved with his family, for better or for worse. Some in-laws are better than others; some you want to hang out with, some you'd rather keep outside of your personal thirty mile zone. It's the luck of the draw.

As the person who knows his family the best, your partner does have a responsibility to act as a buffer between you and Any mama/papa/sister/brother/insert-any-other-family-member drama. Or at the very least give you the heads up. If he's not willing to do this? Warning!

Under circumstances that you won't believe, The Husband's son came to live with us. I'll explain more in another chapter. I was taking care of all of the boy's needs; school, childcare, clothes, everything. Of course, I was given the green light from The Husband to claim his son on my taxes, because he was staying with us full-time. But hold on. Why did it then transpire that Little Man's grandmother, The Ex's mama, was ALSO claiming him on her tax return when he no longer lived with her and was far from an expense for her?

Now here comes the warning: When I told The Husband about this, he did nothing. He didn't call Grandma and tell her to file an amended return, seeing as what she was doing amounted to fraud. Nope, he didn't want any issues with his former in-laws and told me not to worry about it. WHAT???

Again, he put the needs of others before what mattered to us.

Warning after warning after warning after warning.
And still, I stayed.

CHAPTER THREE

When Things Get Real:
Challenges and Changes as a Full Time Momma

"You'd better come and get this little n----- before I kill him."

It was three in the morning when those words were spat down the phone line, shaking The Husband to his core. But the insult wasn't directed at him. The target? His four-year-old son. The source of the vitriol? Little Man's mother.

The Husband's Ex was on the rampage and wanted her young son out of the house. Mother and son found themselves at loggerheads over who knows what and Little Man allegedly put his Mama in a choke hold.

"I think she's drunk," said The Husband, his face etched with confusion and pain. He was trying to process what had just happened while swiftly putting a plan into place to get his boy child to safety. For all the problems he'd experienced with The Ex, this was not a call that he or I were expecting. Yet that call changed our lives in seconds.

The scene that met us at the end of a blurred journey was just pitiful. Little Man looked so small and vulnerable as he slid into the back of the car. He had nothing. No school books, no favorite toys or games, no teddy bear to cuddle at night. Nothing that connected him to his tender years. He was thrown out like a grown adult with little more than the clothes on his back. On our way back home, Little Man said nothing. His mouth refused to betray the turmoil of his heart. He was simply quiet, but his face spoke volumes through the silence.

Life changed that night, for all of us. In an instant, Little Man was cast out of the chaotic, yet familiar home he shared with his mom and sisters. The Husband had to grasp quickly what it meant to be a full-time father. And I made the very abrupt transition from a woman who happened to be married to a man with children, to a day-to-day mama with concerns about childcare, PTA meetings and what to cook for dinner. This little boy needed us and I needed to get up to speed fast.

Even though we connected with Little Man once or twice a week, I didn't *know* him beyond the superficial things; his favorite foods, what he was currently studying at school, his favorite sports star. I didn't know about his hopes and fears. I didn't know what kept him awake at night. I didn't know his weaknesses and strengths.

Getting Little Man settled in that first night, it became clear that life would never be the same again. We had a handful of clothes in the house from some of his past visits, but buying pants and shirts and shoes to shield his tiny frame was easy. Taking on the responsibility for Little Man's physical and mental well being was a whole other thing.

In his young years he'd already known rejection. He was branded the family's "black sheep" and only ever heard people in his mother's house call him "bad." The rejection ran so deep that Little Man was excluded from a family vacation to Florida with his other siblings. Why? "Well, he's just bad, he doesn't know how to behave" is what we were told.

Little Man's past had to be considered carefully as we plotted the course of "the new normal" around school, homework, reports, extracurricular activities, play dates, family visits and taking care of his day to day needs. In my mind, there was a lot we could get wrong. So often, we all think about the "now" but if you have stepchildren, answer these five questions:

QUESTION ONE: Have you and your partner discussed what would happen if circumstances change and his child has to live with you full-time?

If you answered no, drop this book and have the conversation. **RIGHT NOW**. If your partner has children, even if the likelihood of them coming to live with you is remote, just like any good Girl Scout, be prepared. You don't want to be caught having to tackle difficult questions in the middle of the night while rubbing your eyes and patting down your bed-head hair. Not the best time to make life changing decisions.

Ask yourself - if something happens to the children's mother, are you happy and ready to step in full-time? What impact would it have on your work and your current home life? Do you have the space?

Occasionally, we had conversations about The Husband's three children living with us. He had ongoing concerns about their mother's lifestyle choices and the whole situation bothered him. But there was a problem: the Husband didn't have his own home, so he was reliant on me to provide a suitable arrangement to accommodate all of us. At the time we were living in a one bedroom duplex, so having the children with us just wasn't feasible. Yet when we found ourselves rescuing Little Man in the middle of the night, we had to make it work as best we could.

QUESTION TWO: If the children come to live with you, how will household responsibilities be divided?

A woman's work is never done and, with children in the mix, there's always more to do. We have the day to day of getting them up, dressed, fed and at the school gate on time for class. Then there's helping with homework and special projects. Add to that laundry, cooking and housework, play dates with friends, visits with family, after-school programs, sports and other extracurricular activities. I can tell you're already exhaling hard with exhaustion just thinking about it. How will you and your partner divide the labor?

Just by virtue of the fact that you're female, you may put pressure on yourself to create a perfect home environment. And even though this immersion into motherhood is sudden, everyone in your house will expect you to have all the answers. The kids may ask, "Where's my homework?" Your husband is likely to inquire, "Have you seen my keys?" You'll barely be able to find your sanity, let alone anything else in those early days. As the new mother, will you be expected to carry the bulk of the household responsibilities? The answer is probably yes!

Let's take a moment for a story to illustrate the need for these questions:

"You're Not My Mommy!" WARNINGS from an Ex-Stepmother

It was springtime in Long Island and Little Man was settling into his new life: a new school, new friends and a chance to play outside and explore. We'd not been in our new home very long when The Husband announced he was heading to New Orleans to sell jewelry during Jazz Fest. After that, he planned to stop at a few other events before heading home. He would be gone for four weeks. Four weeks?!

I'm not going to lie, I was terrified. I would be home alone for the first time with Little Man. I couldn't do a Macaulay Culkin and barricade the house against the bad guys - Little Man wasn't the enemy, he was my stepson! But I had concerns. What if he wouldn't listen to me? How would I discipline him? What if he missed his father? What if he was just flat out bored being around me for such a long period of time? What if I just did everything…wrong?

On our first night in the house together, Little Man decided to test me. We were doing his homework, but he had a "thing" about not redoing sections when it was sloppy or even wrong. At the other end of the scale, I have a "thing" for always giving your best, even when you'd rather just watch TV.

In the midst of the homework stand off, I'd stepped away to take a call from my mother. A few minutes later, I heard Little Man scream, "It's right, it's right. I'm not doing it!"

What?! Little Man was adamant that he was not going to do another stroke of work and it made me so mad. So mad, that before I could think about it, my hand leapt from my side and struck his little body. There was no excuse for it, and I regret striking him to this day. I was frustrated by his father's extended trip, leaving me with bills without contributing a cent to his son's well being in his absence. Everything fell on my shoulders and it was just too much. For example, a babysitter can cost you up to a whopping four hundred dollars a week. How did I end up with everything on my plate?

Because we hadn't discussed how the division of labor would work in practice.

As the slap reverberated around Little Man's body, I ordered him to his room to do his homework and to think about his actions. Moments later he ran down the hallway sobbing, "I want my Mommy!"

Ouch. Now I was on the receiving end of a slapdown – the emotional kind.

My mom was still hanging on the line and heard everything. "Did you hurt him?" she asked. "No," was my shaken response, but I regretted that I'd let loose on him.

Yet every cloud has a silver lining.

With a quiet click of the bedroom door and the sound of light feet padding down the stairs, Little Man appeared with a tear-stained face in the living room and sat on the couch. "I'm ready to work," he said in his small voice. The two of us sat, heads huddled together working through the homework questions one by one until they were done. Just as my mother had done when we were kids, I signed off his homework so that his teacher could see someone cared and was paying close attention. That night, I learned that in order for us to get along, I couldn't be impatient. Little Man learned that doing things half-heartedly just wouldn't fly.

Before that first evening home alone with Little Man, I always felt that my husband was the layer of comfort between us, acting as a cozy buffer that cushioned our fledging relationship. If not for that incident, we may never have connected beyond the common four walls we shared. That night, I got to know him and Little Man got to know me, without the filter of his father or my husband.

I was still left with all of the housework in The Husband's absence and even once he returned, but it was worth it.

QUESTION THREE: What could living with your stepchildren full-time mean for you having your own family?

This can be a tricky one to navigate, but questions have to be asked before you do anything with permanent repercussions. Children are for life and a man who already has commitments in the guise of two or three (or more) children may feel he's done his bit for humanity and is ready to hang up his baby-making boots. This scenario is fine if you already have children, you're happy to take on his children as your own, or you don't feel the desire to bring your own Mini-Me into the world.

But what happens if you DO want to have your own children?

Even though The Husband already had three children, he wanted more. His father had sired eighteen children – yes, I said eighteen – and The Husband so idolized his father that he wanted to prove that the apple doesn't fall far from the tree, as far as seed scattering is concerned.

Pregnancy didn't come easily. We battled through four rounds of IVF, each time pouring ourselves physically and emotionally into the process. For four years we prepared for treatment, we went through treatment, we grieved over the failure of the treatment, then, like insane people, did it all again, until one day, enough was enough.

There was a voice that accompanied every shot, egg retrieval and embryo transfer. "I can raise this baby on my own." Why would a married woman in the midst of throwing thousands into the hands of science in the hope of a God-given miracle think about raising a baby alone? Because I had seen The Husband's failure to truly provide for the family he already had, and I had to reassure myself that bringing a baby into the world with him would work out, no matter what. It perhaps also spoke to the lack of faith I had in him and our marriage.

If having a child means the world to you, make sure you and your partner are on the same page and talking the same language. You don't want to throw away the chance to have your own family for the sake of a man.

QUESTION FOUR: What impact will your stepchildren living with you full time have on your finances?

If it feels as though I talk about finances a lot, it's not that everything is dependent on money, but most things, in some way shape or form, revolve around the acquisition and dispersal of cold hard cash. Children are expensive. It's not their fault; it's simply a reality.

One major expense you may experience if you all live together is a move to a bigger home, whether rented or purchased. Remember I told you that we lived in a one bedroom duplex when Little Man came to live with us? It wasn't an option for us to stay there. Even though he was young and the bedroom was huge, a kid out of diapers shouldn't have to share a bedroom with his parents and certainly not with his dad and his new wife. It's just awkward all around.

For us, the problem was solved by moving to the suburbs of Long Island. I used my own money to put down a deposit and off we went. There was plenty of space, a yard and room for Little Man's friends to come and stay, it was great. That was until I lost my job six months later.

There were many dark days ahead as I hunted, for the first time in my life, to find a new position. The financial sector was hit hard; I was up against people who had also enjoyed job security until it was so rudely snatched away.

The Husband wasn't in a position to pay the mortgage and other expenses because he just didn't earn enough. Instead of putting money in the bank, we were living from my savings and depleting the financial cushion I had so diligently put in place. What choice did we have? If you've not read it already, refer back to the chapter on warnings and what can happen when a man isn't in a position to take care of himself or his children without you.

Suffice to say, it was a stressful time with not just the responsibility of the house, but making sure everything stayed as normal as possible for Little Man. He'd had enough upheaval in his short life and there was no way we could let him get a whiff of the financial problems we were suffering.

Finally, after a six month search for work, the clouds parted and I was back in the land of the gainfully employed. Sweet relief, yes, but the experience took a toll on every one of my last nerves.

I'll talk more about finances and protecting what's yours in a later chapter.

QUESTION FIVE: How much and what type of contact will be you expected to have with the mother?

Speaking of my last nerves, let's talk about dealing with The Ex. Wherever there are stepchildren, there's a mother, aunts, uncles, grandparents and other extended family. In other words, more potential sources of drama. How you deal with them all is something that needs to be addressed and understood from the outset, particularly The Ex.

Are you happy for The Ex to kick it in your home when she visits the children? Will you be expected to keep her in the loop with certain family plans? How will you fit in to pick up and drop off plans? What power do you have when it comes to making decisions for your stepchild?

Let's address one issue: The Drop Off.

Since The Husband had sole custody of his son, every weekend we had the chance of dropping off and collecting Little Man from his mother. One Sunday afternoon, I was on a drive with my niece which was meant to end with us picking Little Man up from his mother's house. If you know New York then you know the ten mile commute from Long Island to Brooklyn is over an hour on a good day. We were talking, playing music and having fun, so the drive didn't feel long, but drama met us at the end.

It was summertime, so The Ex and some of her family members were sitting outside trying to catch some cool air. They're not the friendliest of people and I was truly intimidated pulling up, but tried to keep it light and breezy. There had been previous occasions where alcohol turned a perfectly normal situation into all out war.

Little Man saw me, I said, "Hi," and asked him if he was ready to go.

Before he had time to answer, his mother called, "Come here."

I thought nothing of it - after all, Little Man is her son. They disappeared into the house. Five minutes turned to ten minutes turned to twenty minutes turned to an hour. And still we waited. I had no idea why they went in the house or why he was in there so long.

Perhaps he was finishing some homework. Perhaps he was doing a job for his mother. Perhaps The Ex was just being difficult in making me wait so long.

I called The Husband, "I've been waiting outside for Little Man for an hour. Can you call his mother and remind her that I'm out here?" The Husband said he called her and she knew I was waiting. And still we waited. Almost two hours went by. Nothing.

A friend who lived across the street asked me what I was doing there so long. I said I was waiting for my stepson, but his mother had not come out with him. "She's a bad person," he said. Bad person or not, I reached the end of my rope. Little Man wasn't the problem. Dealing with The Ex's hostility was and I wasn't prepared to play. So I left. This was officially above my pay grade.

I made the drive from Long Island to Brooklyn often to drop off and collect Little Man. Not once did The Ex get on the train and bring him home. After the nonsense with The Ex, I had to ask myself - why was I doing all of this extra work? I had to put up with hostility, in addition to a long drive for zero thanks and no back up from The Husband. It made no sense. So I stopped.

You have to be clear on what is expected of you and how much you want to give, because dealing with The Ex may not be the easiest way to spend your weekend.

Pick ups aside, you also have issues surrounding what we'll call "child admin." Let's take, for example, school pictures. Everyone loves the annual tradition, where you see the little people grow up; marking the transition from childhood to adulthood through pearly whites and ever-changing hairstyles.

Even though the relationship between Little Man and his mother was strained, I wanted to keep her a part of his Monday to Friday life in Long Island. I mean, what mother doesn't want a lasting image of their child to look at?

So I made a point of ordering extra copies for her and Little

Man was happy that his Mommy would have a picture of him. As I dropped him off for the weekend, I presented The Ex with the picture package, Little Man's beaming smile bouncing off the photo paper. He even signed the back to make it even more personal. I truly thought she would be happy and would make a big deal out of looking at the shots. She didn't. Instead she talked about so many unimportant things, which had nothing to do with the handsome young man in the picture.

Eventually, I drove off and she left the picture right there on the passenger seat. The Ex didn't try to flag down my car. She didn't call me or The Husband to ask us to send it on to her. Nor did she ask about the picture on subsequent drop offs. I cried so hard for Little Man on the drive home, for the thoughtlessness of his own mother and her dismissive treatment of him. That, in addition to everything else, made me want to be an even better stepmother to him. Sadly, no matter how she treated him, Little Man would always seek his mother's approval and pine for her love and affection.

The number of challenging circumstances you'll find yourself in as a stepmother are endless. But once you make the decision to dive in, you have to be *all* in. No matter how difficult the relationship is with The Ex, the child has to be at the front and center of all of your interactions. Your stepchild will look at this relationship and perceive any hostility between the two of you as a reflection of how his "two mamas" feel about him.

If this life isn't for you, if you're not willing to fight just as hard for a child who isn't your blood relative, walk away now. If you decide to move ahead, know that the road gets even tougher as you try to build and maintain a relationship with your stepchild while protecting your own finances and feelings.

This is why early conversations on how you will incorporate a stepchild into your life are crucial. There's too much at stake for everyone involved.

CHAPTER FOUR

No Romance Without Finance: Babies, Budgets and Bank Balances

Allow me a moment of indulgence as I take the scenic route to make a point, which will all make sense in a few moments. Whether you're a parent or not, you've witnessed this scene: two toddlers are playing together. They both eye a favorite toy. They slowly look up at one another like two gunfighters at the OK Corral. On the count of three, two sets of chubby hands lunge towards the toy, locking onto the object at the same time.

With no desire to back down, a tug of war ensues, both parties clinging on for dear life, reluctant to let go until one of them has sole possession. Left to their own devices, the children would figure this out. One would get a beatdown, the other would move on to the next thing. After all, children have the attention span of a fruit fly.

Not wanting their child to look selfish and anti-social, one parent smiles through gritted teeth and says "Bobby, you must learn to share," in a mock sing-song voice. The toy is pried out of the pulsating palm of one of the toddlers, whose world crashes down in front of him as the toy floats over to his opponent. Victory is washed away through a sea of tears and the devastating crash of defeat. Mommy becomes the traitor. Thanks Mom.

Now you may be asking, "What have two warring toddlers got to do with being a stepmother?" Well, children share great wisdom when it comes to how we adults should approach the world and here's one such lesson for anyone contemplating step-motherhood: sharing isn't always a good thing. Sometimes it doesn't feel nice. And it's okay to keep what you have for yourself.

What we're talking about here is money. Dinero, bread, dough, bucks, Benjamins - cold, hard cash. Dollar bills (the lack or misappropriation of) are the root of many a marital meltdown. If you have a little, you want more. If you're maintaining, you keep a watchful eye on your spending. And if you have a lot, you want to keep hold of it.

So here's a question: Why, when we enter into a relationship, do we want to share everything, including the contents of our bank accounts? This is a complicated enough question, but when you add the dynamics of stepparenthood, it goes to another level. What's mine is yours and what's yours is mine, right?

Before we proceed, I need to make this clear. Financial problems as a stepmother are in no way the fault of the child. Yes, if your partner's children live with you, there are additional daily expenses that you wouldn't have as a single woman, but feeding an extra mouth or two shouldn't be an issue. You'd feed your own children or any other child in your home, so it should be no different for your stepchildren.

What we're talking about in this chapter are the hidden expenses and financial drains that can take place if honest questions aren't asked that can prevent exposing you to the risk of losing whatever you bring monetarily in to the relationship.

People don't like talking about money; what we earn, how much we owe, what we spend on rent and housing. This reluctance to share financial information in a relationship can spell disaster. Don't be shy. Asking difficult questions now will save you so much more later.

If you're stuck for a place to start a financial pow-wow with your loved one, here's the first question:

QUESTION ONE: What do you observe?

I loved to watch The Husband with his children. He was playful, thoughtful, loving, sweet and totally engaged with their needs in the moment. They were all smiles and laughter; to the casual observer, The Husband was the picture of fatherly love and tenderness.

Comparing notes with another stepmother friend, there's nothing better than seeing a man with his children. On a basic "survival of the species" level, seeing a man care for his own child validates a woman's choice in a mate, encouraging her to procreate even more. However, by getting caught up in the beauty of seeing our men interact with their progeny, it's easy to overlook one crucial thing: how are they taking care of them financially? In my case, the answer was - he wasn't. He couldn't. And he had no plan to change that.

When we first met, The Husband's three children lived with their mother who made a career out of being on welfare. There is nothing wrong with being on welfare, but there is something wrong with not using the help you receive to make sure your children are properly cared for. The children, who were really just babies when The Husband and I first connected, would often arrive for visits unkempt, unwashed and in clothes that hadn't seen laundry detergent for weeks. The sight of these children was beyond pitiful.

One day, I went with The Husband to collect the kids for the weekend. All of them came out to the car with no coats. That would be fine if we lived in the perpetual sunshine of Southern California, but snow and freezing temperatures are a staple of brutal New York winters.

There's more. Back at his mother's, The Husband's son was forced to sleep on the sofa because his room was being used by "a friend." He would return from visits to his mom's house with what looked like bug bites all over his little body.

All of these things broke The Husband's heart. Yet no matter how pained he felt by the situation, his financial problems meant he was powerless to change anything. He scrapped together a living, didn't have his own place, didn't have a car and he had no medical benefits. Herein lies the problem:

If a man doesn't have the financial means to look after his own children BEFORE the two of you get together, what do you think will change once he's married or living full-time with you?

I knew long before we married that we should probably part ways on the basis of one observation. As an executive working in finance in Manhattan I was often invited to events, some work related, many not. One day, my boss asked the team to his country club for a private holiday party. It's never spoken of, but the expectation is that people will dress to impress for these occasions: a suit for men and elegant attire for the women. In an off-handed comment to The Husband, I said, "Hey, you need to wear a suit to the country club." The reply? "I don't have one." *I don't have one??*

Even if you're fortunate enough to wear casual clothes to the office on a daily basis, lurking somewhere in your closet is a suit, the one dragged out for weddings, funerals, job interviews and any other life occasion which requires a level of effort above jeans and a t-shirt. But he didn't own one. Okay, fine. But he didn't have the financial means to go out and buy one either. In other words, The Husband was not in a position to look after himself. Which demonstrated clearly that he couldn't care for his children. Not because he didn't want to, but because he couldn't. And still, I stayed (and yes, I bought him a suit.)

QUESTION TWO: What financial ties and obligations does your partner have to his ex and children?

When a man has children with another woman, they are tied forever and, as much as you may not like it, there's nothing you can do about it. This is a bond you have to make peace with and respect as best you can.

However, there are financial implications that will impact you directly and you need to be prepared.

The fallout from The Husband's relationship with his ex hit my household in two key ways that I did not see coming.

First, The Husband owed child support. A lot of it. He gave his three children what he could from the proceeds of his business, but the work was not consistent, with money coming in some weeks, then nothing the next. Yet he was reluctant to get a full time job to put us in a better position to bring all of his children to live with us. The Husband knew his wages would be garnished. He preferred to remain financially reliant on his wife rather than do what he needed to do to help us move forward and secure a better life for his children. He was depressed and angry, but not enough to do anything about it.

When The Husband's son came to live with us, another financial complication came to the surface.

Little Man needed a lot of medical attention - his immunization record was incomplete for school and his teeth were in bad shape. At the age of four he already had cavities. Even though his mother received government aid, which entitled them to free medical and dental treatment, the documentation was nowhere to be found. Little Man's medical card was lost and every time The Husband asked for it, there was some excuse as to why is wasn't available. In the meantime, Little Man still needed to be cared for.

Tired of the back and forth with The Husband's ex, I put Little Man on my company benefits so he could get the care he needed. I didn't want to step out of turn, but what was I to do? Leave Little Man and let all of his teeth fall out of his head? We didn't share DNA, but I saw no reason why I shouldn't care for Little Man as my own.

Even though you may not want to put a dollar figure on the basics of health, the reality is that these costs have to come out of a money pot somewhere. Are you willing and able to do this?

QUESTION THREE: Who is responsible for sourcing and providing childcare for your stepchild?

Depending on where your stepkids are in the childhood cycle, the issue of childcare may or may not be relevant to you. If you have a teenager, you have other concerns such as discipline, curfews and reasoning with a person who is fast becoming an adult with ideas and proclivities of his own. For those who are involved with a man with younger children, read on.

When it comes to childcare, where do the boundaries lie for a stepmother? Should you be responsible for organizing daycare, a nanny or a babysitter? Just how much should this be your concern and should you be responsible for paying for it?

The answer? It depends on your situation and what the expectations are within your relationship. We go back to that all-important question. Did the two of you discuss it?

The Husband's son came to live with us after that "tussle" with his mother. He arrived in the middle of the night draped only with the clothes on his tiny back. Once we moved out of the one bedroom duplex we shared in Queens to a spacious house in Long Island, it became evident that we needed help. The Husband was often out of town on business, so while he was away it was just Little Man and me.

As a woman without children, I really had no idea just how much childcare cost. Being a stay at home stepmother was not an option and Little Man's own mom wasn't interested in looking after him beyond his weekly visits. Little Man's extended family didn't live close enough to help either. On the odd occasion, members of my family who live on Long Island watched him but this wasn't something I could rely on. Plus it felt wrong asking them for help.

When The Husband travelled out of town, my day would start at five a.m. I'd get Little Man up, dressed and fed before dropping him at the babysitter so I could make it to work in Manhattan on time. After school, the babysitter would collect Little Man and watch him until I returned home. This service cost $400 a week – the equivalent of another mortgage. I had no issue finding good childcare for Little Man, but I did have a problem with me pulling the funds out of my own pocket.

QUESTION FOUR: If something was to happen to your partner, what financial provisions are in place to take care of his children?

Believe me when I say this, I'm really not trying to scare you with this chapter and present a picture of impending doom and gloom when it comes to stepmotherhood. There are some uncomfortable truths about living life, and sadly, death is one of them. The loss of a loved one can be one of the most expensive parts of life if you're not prepared.

I'm a sentimental being and the passing of those close to me leaves a hole in my soul. Yet as a finance professional I'm all about arming yourself with contingency plans should the worst happen.

Due to The Husband's financial situation, I took out a life

insurance policy for him and another one for Little Man once he was living with us. I can see some of your faces saying, "Isn't that weird, taking out life insurance on a kid?"

The reality is this: if something happened to Little Man, who was going to pay for his funeral? Even the most simple of ceremonies, if you're not donating your body to science, will run into thousands of dollars.

I didn't want there to be any confusion if Little Man died, with his mother or father begging for handouts to lay their own child to rest. He deserved better than that. Was it my place to do so? Yes. As a financially responsible adult, I felt I had little choice if I wanted to ensure the little one had a good send off, but selfishly, I didn't want to wrack up mountains of debt, given that I knew neither of his parents had a dime.

In the case of The Husband, the reasoning was slightly different. Yes, I wanted to make sure the prohibitive costs of his home-going were covered, but I also wanted to secure some financial stability for his children. The policy ensured that each child would have enough to use for college or as a down payment for a home once they were of age.

I remember how I felt when my own father passed and left nothing for his children. It's not about the money, it's about feeling that you were thought of. I wanted The Husband's children to feel cherished enough to be cared for, even if their father was gone. Needless to say, The Husband wasn't happy about it. I guess he realized he was worth more to me dead than alive.

QUESTION FIVE: Should I sign a pre-nup?

Thanks to Hollywood starlets, the prenuptial agreement has achieved mystical status among "ordinary" people such as us. Don't pretend you weren't interested in the details of TomKat's pre wedding paperwork (yes, we're all glad she got Suri!)

Yet prenups, from a financial point of view, can be good for everybody, especially when you've worked hard to accumulate assets which you're not quite ready to throw into the communal money pot. "But pre-nups aren't exactly romantic, are they?" Well, no they're not, but there's nothing romantic about being broke after a divorce either.

The other benefit to bringing up the question of a prenuptial agreement is that it forces you both to lay out -- in no uncertain terms -- what you have and what's coming with you should you part ways. You're not looking into a crystal ball and predicting failure, but rather taking a proactive step to securing both of your futures should circumstances change. This is crucial where children are involved.

Divorce is upsetting enough for all involved without throwing an argument about money onto the smoldering embers of a dying marriage.

So the advice is simple: If you have more to lose than you can afford to give away, get a prenup. If your partner is offended by the idea, or won't entertain a prenup, walk away. He probably has hidden motives anyway.

QUESTION SIX: But I should let him drive my car though, right? That's harmless enough...

Let's go back to my opening scenario with the toddlers refusing to share. Sometimes it's good *not* to share, no matter what your mother told you.

God has been good to me. I have a great job, enjoy foreign travel and have been fortunate enough to work in an industry where generous bonuses and pay raises were the norm. With these extra payouts I've been able to invest in projects, work towards a financially secure future and even splurge a little.

One year I bought myself a car outright, with no monthly payments. It really felt like a gift from above, so I took great care of my new wheels. That's what you do with presents from people, right?

The Husband didn't have good credit, didn't own a car, but really needed one to get to and from his events and also to collect the children when they came to stay with us. It was a no-brainer for me to give him that car while I took on a new car payment for myself.

When I gave him the car, it was literally brand new. Within months the car interior stank to high heaven and was deplorable beyond belief. Worse still, The Husband racked up thousands of dollars worth of parking tickets, which of course he couldn't and didn't pay. The tickets were worth more than the car's value when it was impounded, so the car was sold at auction.

If that wasn't enough, The Husband then got caught driving without his license, not once, but three times. Each time he called me. Each time I bailed him out to the tune of five hundred dollars. One time I asked my mother if she could help out, as I was short on immediate funds. She looked at me like I'd lost my mind. Needless to say, she said no to posting bail and told me to get his mother to bail him out.

Why did he feel it was okay to do this? Because he had no respect for money and even less respect for mine. If you've never had to work hard for what you have, how could you?

The warning here is that you must observe how your partner acts with his own. Actions speak so much louder than words.

Watch what he's telling YOU.

CHAPTER FIVE

The Emotional Rollercoaster:
Guarding Your Heart in the Ups and Downs of Love

If you're a woman of a tender disposition, wipe off your mascara, grab yourself some tissues and take a seat. We're about to get emotional.

Unless you're one of life's truly blessed women who has never experienced the loss of a loved one or the brutal end to a once promising intimate relationship, then you will know how it feels to have your feelings hurt and your emotions trampled. It's not the kind of hurt that anyone can see, touch or hear. It's a hurt that you wear like a second skin, so tight that you almost can't breathe, but take it off and your vulnerability is there in plain view for all to see.

When it comes to matters of the heart as a stepmother, you don't need a second skin. You need full combat body armor to survive what could be an emotional battlefield. You see, if you love your man, you will love his children. Yes, that's true even if they get on your last nerve or you never thought of yourself as the maternal type. It may not happen overnight, but it will happen.

With The Husband's children, it happened at different times and in different ways. With his son, it was from the moment I first saw him, all doe-eyed and shy with the most brilliant smile. I felt like Alice in Wonderland tumbling down the rabbit hole: once I stuck my head in, I just kept falling and falling and falling. With the daughters, it was a longer process over many meetings, but I miss them to this day. They weren't my blood children, but my desire to protect them and fight for them was just as strong as if they were my own.

So what are the emotional crunch points stepmothers and stepmothers-to-be need to look out for? And just how can you guard your heart to save it from damage caused by those emotional bumps in the road?

CRUNCH POINT 1: The (umbilical) ties that bind

I have to start with what is completely obvious, but where many stepmothers come undone before they even begin. Remember this: children will always think more of their mother than they do of you. That's just how it is.

Think about your own mother for a moment. Whether the two of you have a great relationship or one that's on more of a special days and birthdays basis, the chances are you at least acknowledge her for giving you life. There is a lifelong bond between mothers and their children that is not so easily broken. The physical umbilical cord may be long gone, but the spiritual connection remains for a lifetime.

My stepson frequently reminded me of the forever bond he shares with his mother, even though her actions made it clear she didn't want him. On special occasions, he spent hours crafting beautiful cards with his own little hands; stickers, glue, glitter and tissue paper spread across the table and shaped by his busy fingers. Later, he'd pick the freshest flowers he could find before proudly presenting his mommy with the gift. No amount of effort was too much.

By contrast, Little Man never did that for me, even though we lived in the same house and shared laughs, meals, prayers and a life. Ultimately, his mommy had all of his heart, even if she didn't hold him in hers. It was not a competition for affection, he rightfully wanted to show his mother love. Regardless, I would always lose and it always hurt.

Children will never set out to intentionally hurt your feelings, but as a stepmother, you have to steel your emotions for Mother's Day, birthdays, Christmas and other holidays, because you will come low on the list of priorities when it comes to doing anything thoughtful and special. Just remember they are children and the pull of the umbilical cord is strong, far-reaching and eternal.

What can you do to ease the pain? On these crunch days, plan something special for yourself; a spa day, or a day out with another stepmother friend. If you'd like to keep things family-oriented, suggest an evening at the movies or check out a local theme park. Every day, you have the opportunity to build memories in your stepchild's life that include you. They'll remember those moments fondly, even if they don't remember to make you a card.

CRUNCH POINT 2: Words Hurt

I'm sure you recall this school yard rhyme:

Sticks and stones may break my bones, but names will never hurt me.

"You're Not My Mommy!" WARNINGS from an Ex-Stepmother

Er, no, that's not true. Words *do* hurt. Words cut deep and take longer to heal than any physical wound.

We've all had those fights with friends, family, partners, where words tumble out of our mouths only to crack at the feet of the person on the receiving end. What follows is the silence of a mind processing what just happened: somewhere in the middle of that silence, you'll hear a thud. That's the sound of your words damaging a little piece of your sparring partner's heart.

If you're a stepmother, you will experience this many times, but you must guard against forming tough calluses over your emotions. Protecting yourself shouldn't come at the expense of tenderness.

The most common phrase to damage a stepmother is:

You're Not My Mommy!

These words are often accompanied by pouting, foot stamping and slammed doors and can be brought on by everything from an innocent request to help with the dishes to more serious disciplinary action. Either way, being reminded that you are not the mommy is enough to hurt even the toughest woman.

Little Man said this to me once, and it cut me to the core. It was in the middle of a heated conversation about school work, and he screamed, "I want my mommy!" and ran off like a sulky teenager to his room. It stopped me in my tracks. After everything, he still wanted her.

Tackling this particular brand of hurt is difficult, but you have to remember that you are the adult in this situation. Fighting hurtful words with hurtful words is pointless and under no circumstances should an adult enter into emotional combat with a child.

Instead, remove yourself from the situation and take a breath. Focus on all the good in the relationship with your stepchild. Once you're calm, consider having a conversation with him, pointing out that you know you're not his mother, but you love him as if he were your own and you want to help him feel better and safe and secure. You may have to repeat this many times, but if you're in it for the long haul, letting your stepchild know you love him and will always be there will pay dividends in years to come.

CRUNCH POINT 3: What's my name?

There's a whole chapter that could be written on what a stepchild should call their stepmother. Mommy? Mommy [insert your name]? Just address you by your first name? Something else?

A name is a name right? Well in this case, no. For some women, there's a direct correlation between how they're addressed and where they fall on the sliding scale of affection. If they call you Mommy, you're a keeper! If they call you by your first name, perhaps they don't see you as a permanent feature in their lives. If they call you nothing at all? You have bigger communication issues to tackle.

My stepchildren called me Donna. I didn't like it, but their father offered them no guidance on how to address me. You have to remember, this is a big deal for children. They will always remain loyal to their mother, and may feel strange having two mothers. You have to give them time to process the situation and come up with what makes them comfortable.

In my case, it's not that I wanted to be called Mommy, but having children address me by my first name as if we were equals didn't sit well. It was as if I was a side to their lives and not a true part of it. As the years went by I learned to deal with it, but I felt I was more to them than just "Donna," especially to Little Man.

If you are addressed by your first name and this is what your stepchildren feel most comfortable with, don't force it. In this instance, you have to swallow any hurt and smile through the pain. As your relationship deepens and they get to know you better, there may come a day when "Mommy" spills naturally from their tongues. Don't make a big deal out of it. By this point, calling you "Mom" is no longer a problem and they've reconciled any loyalty conflict they previously had.

If you can, discuss the naming protocol with your partner as soon as you feel comfortable doing so. Opening the conversation with him may ease the path to a naming convention that is natural for everyone. In the meantime, don't be offended if they chose to call you by your first name. It is, after all, the name you were given.

CRUNCH POINT 4: Uncomfortable sightings

I have one wish for every stepmother: That she has a decent relationship with her partner's baby mama. It's no fun for any kid to see their mother arguing, let alone exchanging harsh words with another woman who is also a mother figure in her life.

Yet disagreement is part of living. The challenge as a stepmother is knowing how aggressively to step in when you see something you deem as a problem for your stepchild.

I had real issues with how The Ex was raising her children. Sometimes we'd collect the kids from their mother and they looked unkempt and uncared for. The Husband often complained that their homework was incomplete - that's if they attempted to do it at all. Of course we were a daily presence in Little Man's life, but only saw the daughters on occasion. We did what we could whenever they stayed with us, but it just underlined the powerlessness of The Husband's situation. And he felt it.

As a stepmother, you have feelings for your stepchildren and no one likes to see a child going through drama, no matter the source. It's difficult to set boundaries on where your involvement begins and ends, especially if the source of the problem is the children's mother.

If this is the case, the first port of call should be the father, your partner. Is he aware of the issues you have seen? How receptive will he be to you sharing your observations? Get this wrong and you could stir up emotional flares between you and your partner. What if he ignores what you say? What will you do then?

Ultimately, you have to do what you think is right and what will help you sleep at night. If you see something you don't agree with and you feel you can, speak up.

Your partner's response could tell you so much more about the state of your relationship than anything else.

CRUNCH POINT 5: Divorce

No one wants to talk about divorce when they've only just gotten together, but with one in three marriages ending Tammy Wynette style, we can't discuss life as a stepmother without broaching the subject.

The reality is, relationships come to an end for all manner of reasons; they run their course, your partner turns out to not be who you thought he was; you grow apart; your partner cheats on you. The possibilities are endless.

Discovering that your husband has cheated on you is one of the most soul-destroying things that can happen to a human being. This person that you trusted more than any other, the person who you vowed to love and cherish until the end of your days, decides he'd also like to sample some goods elsewhere "just in case." A decade of love and friendship done, finished, over.

The tears I cried over the end of my marriage were nothing compared to the rivers that flowed over losing my stepchildren. I was so attached to Little Man, that even when I realized our relationship was over, I still tried to find ways for us to stay together as a family. Not for the sake of my marriage, but for the sake of the child. I even suggested that Little Man continue to live with me so he could finish his education at the school he so loved and where he thrived. But here comes the emotional kicker:

The Ex said, "He's my child, he's coming with me. You're not his mother." What could I say to that? The children *weren't* mine. As a stepmother, you have no legal standing, no right to claim the kids as your own. With the swipe of a court judge's pen, once the ink on your divorce is final, you are no longer a part of their lives. Even though you will always be a part of their history, you won't feature in their future.

This realization was made all the more painful by the struggles we'd had trying to conceive. IVF failed to give us a biological child together and it made me even more grateful for the relationship I had with my stepchildren.

How can you guard you heart against the fallout of a divorce and the removal of the little people from your life? Honestly, you can't. You just have to learn to live with it.

The emotional battlefield of stepmotherhood is one you will navigate every day; dealing with your partner, his ex, your stepchildren and other family members. At every step you have to remind yourself of why you are there.

It never hurts to have strategies to protect yourself. Here are a few:

- *Don't take harsh words from your stepchildren personally. Develop your own relationship with them built on respect and understanding.*

- *Don't expect miracles overnight. Rome wasn't built in a day and love doesn't happen overnight.*

- *Discuss your emotional concerns with your partner. He may be able to help.*

- *If the two of you are heading for divorce, try to find a way to keep in contact with the stepchildren in a way that everyone concerned agrees on. Perhaps through cards, text message or a shared interest, such as sporting events, the movies or underwater basketweaving – whatever you and your stepchild traditionally do together*

- *Remember, you will never be number one with your stepchildren – but number three isn't a terrible place to be either.*

CHAPTER SIX

The Case of the Ex: How to Avoid Baby-mama Drama

As Sly famously sang in 1971, *"'It's a Family Affair."* In this case the family refers to you, your husband, his children - and his ex. That's a lot of family, and we haven't even made it to the in-laws yet.

As a stepmother and the latest addition to your Brady-esque bunch, you can expect to do much of the heavy lifting when it comes to creating what will become "the new normal." This will include playing nice with The Ex and creating ground rules that will prevent an all-out war between the two of you. Grown- ups misbehave too. Remember, no matter what, as the adults you ALL have to set a good example to the children involved in this complicated family dynamic.

So how do you get on the path to good ex-wife/new wife relations? Before you can start this journey, you need to consider how your husband and his ex parted ways. If the spilt was an amicable we-just-grew-apart situation, The Ex is likely to be open to getting to know you, if only on a superficial level. You'll exchange social pleasantries and phone numbers and she may even invite you in for a glass of water without feeling the need to lace it with bug killer. A win-win for all concerned.

On the other hand, if they didn't part ways on the best of terms, for example he called time on their marriage, don't expect a warm handshake and an offer to stay for dinner. Or if she does offer, you may want to pass. Do I need to remind you of the saying, "Hell hath no fury like a woman scorned"?

You're a visual representation of what she doesn't have: The Husband. In the ex's mind, you are the source of her unhappiness and the wrecker of her happy home, even if you had nothing to do with their breakup and they were miserable together for years. Of course, this is a generalization, but we've all been on the receiving end of hurt and it can be difficult to summon up the desire to be warm, kind and reasonable while your heart is breaking.

Once "'the breakup'" story has been established, you can begin to consider the rules of engagement for this new relationship - the one between you and the former Mrs.. You also have to get through the first official meeting.

In my case, it didn't go well. Before I laid eyes on The Husband's ex, I had a *feeling*. The waters were not happy. One evening as we dropped the children home, The Ex was outside playing ball with some friends. The Husband introduced us from a distance, possibly to prevent any chance of physical contact or an ill timed choke hold. Perhaps he knew that her default setting was "hostile."

As he called our names, I felt an icy hostility of Arctic proportions blowing in my direction. The anger was so intense, my mind conjured up an image of her, wide-eyed and head tilted, sliding an imaginary knife across her neck while mouthing, "I'm gonna get you," in my direction. The Ex was very clearly not on Team Donna.

Suffice to say, we never enjoyed an easy relationship. I didn't expect us to be BFF's, but I was thrown by the level of dislike I was getting from The Ex. She knew nothing about me. My experience with The Ex is not unique.

Whether the relationship with your husband's ex starts on a good foot or a bum note, the two of you have to find a way to interact that will be comfortable for everyone involved, especially in three key areas:

AREA ONE: The Drop Off

One of the main mother/child/stepmother interactions comes at collection and drop off time. These moments can be tough for children as they're saying goodbye to one parent and may feel a level of guilt for having had a good time in their mother's absence.

It can also be an emotionally fraught time for the adults, just ask Halle Berry. Gabriel Aubry, the father of her daughter and her fiancé, Oliver Martinez got into a punch-up while Mini Berry was being dropped off for Thanksgiving in 2012. The adults have since come to an amicable agreement, but not before a couple of black eyes, busted ribs, a sore hand and some bruised egos.

Before things get physical, it's best to come up with a set of rules for how the drop off/collection will be done, especially if you as the stepmother will handle this the most.

In my situation, I chose not to enter The Ex's house when dropping the children off. It reduced the risk of any cross words between us and created a safe transition space for the children to say goodbye to me before entering her home. Of course, this didn't always go according to plan.

I loved to spoil my stepchildren, especially for their birthdays. One year, I took the eldest daughter on a New York shopping spree, complete with lunch at her favorite restaurant and topped off with a runway fashion show featuring the shoes we bought at a local boutique. We laughed and joked and had the best time.

It being her birthday, we'd agreed to take her back to her mother's house to continue the festivities with the rest of her family. What a lucky young girl to be celebrated the whole day with two families who love her very much!

As was our custom, we drove to her mother's house; I chose to wait in the car while The Husband took his eldest daughter indoors. As any young girl would, she recreated her fashion show and twirled and danced for the family wearing her new threads.

I knew my husband would be a while, so I called my sister to catch up. Moments later, I heard a knock on my window. "Get out the car. I heard you were talking about me." It was The Ex.

My first instinct was to fling open the door and punch her so hard that she could only see cartoon birds circling above. The quiet voice in my head - in this case, my sister - told me to be the bigger person.

With an intake of breath, I slowly opened the car door and deliberately planted one foot on the ground. Adrenaline still had me in fight mode, so the usually mindless act of getting out of the car became an exercise in mind over body. As I turned to free my second foot, finger by finger I unclenched my fist. Feet secure, I unfurled my five feet eight inch frame until I was upright. Only then did I notice that The Ex's family had come out in force to catch a girl fight. What broke my heart, was my stepdaughter, dressed in her finery, crying hysterically, begging her mother to stop.

What if I'd responded to The Ex's heat with even more fire? I would have damaged the delicate relationship with my eldest stepdaughter for good and failed as a role model for all of my stepchildren. I walked away unscathed, but sad, not for me, but for my stepdaughter. That's a birthday she will never forget, but not for the right reasons.

So the question is, how do you deal with drop offs to avoid physical altercations and verbal attacks?

- *Keep the transition time from one parent to another as short as possible.*

You don't have to push the children out of the car with the motor running, but you also don't need to invite yourself in, kick off your heels and relax on the couch. Long transitions are confusing for the children and offer the opportunity for awkward conversations to start.

- *Agree on the day and time for collection and drop off and stick to it.*

I'm not saying you have to adhere to times with military precision, but if the day and time are set in stone, there's no excuse for the children not to be where they're meant to be because a parent or stepparent forgot. Paper and digital calendars make it easy to remember appointments. If you're running late for any reason and your relationship with The Ex allows, let her know yourself. Don't get one of the kids to call.

- *Consult the children.*

If they're old enough, the children may prefer to make their own way to and from their mother's house. Have the conversation, make sure all parties agree and move forward with the plan.

- *Don't force yourself into a space where you're not welcome.*

If you have a less than amicable relationship with the mother, you may not be the best person to do the pick up and drop off. Speak with your husband or another family member who may be better suited to take care of this.

AREA TWO: Holidays and Special Occasions

Thanksgiving. Christmas. Independence Day. Birthdays. Anniversaries. Weddings. Mother's Day. Father's Day. Vacations. There are hundreds of special days and events that bring families together, but which need to be handled with care by stepmothers.

Some children may see the benefit to having two families; that's double the gifts and double the fun! For others, it's a reminder that their parents are no longer together and they may have difficulty navigating these occasions without a sense of loss or guilt. Two Christmas dinners is not everyone's idea of a good time.

As the stepmother, how can you help?

- *Plan joint events*

If relations are amicable, consider hosting some occasions jointly, such as a child's birthday party. This would give you an opportunity to work with the mother to create something special where both of you share goal: a great day for the little Mr. or Miss.

- *Plan ahead*

At a time that suits all of you, sit down and go over plans for the year - vacations, birthdays, graduations and events that fall outside of your designated time that you would like the children to attend. Also go over key dates like the holiday season and Thanksgiving and devise a plan that works for you all. If you can't agree, consider backing down. This isn't about you, it's about the children.

- *Keep the mother in the loop*

If the children live with you, make sure The Ex knows about school events: PTA meetings, sporting contests, music recitals, plays. Give her the opportunity to participate, especially if she doesn't live in the same town or has to give advance notice at work.

- *Send cards and pictures*

In an effort to build relations with your husband's ex, consider including her on your card list. A Happy Birthday note or Thanksgiving wish can go a long way. If the children live with you, make sure they send cards or help them choose or make a gift for their mother. Post in plenty of time if she lives far away. Children will forget!

Not all mother's will be open to these efforts to build a relationship and efforts to keep her connected to her own children may not be appreciated. Still, make the effort. No-one can never say you didn't try.

AREA THREE: Maintaining Rules and Routines

Everyone has an opinion on how children should be raised, especially when it comes to rules, routines and the big D: Discipline. To spank or not to spank; to time out or not to time out; to remove privileges or try to reason. These are just a handful of discipline questions to address.

This becomes more complicated when the cast of characters involved in raising a child extends beyond Mom and Dad.

As a stepparent, how much say do you get when it comes to discipline? How could implementing rules impact on your relationship with the mother?

In my case, there was very little cross over or communication with the mother of The Husband's children, so in many ways I was fortunate to be able to develop rules and routines that worked in our home for Little Man who lived with us full time and for his sisters when they came to visit. Even in this case, it's difficult to know how far you can go. Is it okay to raise a hand to someone else's child, even if they are in your care part of the time? Is it okay to have a different set of rules if they only spend part of the time with you?

With both of these issues, consistency is key for children. It will soon become confusing if they have to follow two sets of rules in two different households. And while physical punishment may be okay for you, it may not be okay with their mother.

The steps to take here to maintain good relations with the mother are straightforward:

- *Consult first. Establish the ground rules.*

This is a matter that must be discussed with all the adults involved in your stepchild's life, even if you all don't get along. Make a list of the rules that apply in both houses and put it in plain view for your stepchildren to see. That way they can't try to play one household off against another.

- *Let your husband take the lead.*

The children are, after all, his, and he will be the constant figure between the two homes. The children will know that he knows what they can and can't do. Also, when it comes to discipline, they're likely to listen to him and act on his words. Given time, they will listen to you too, but this is a relationship that will take a while to build.

- *When in doubt, ask.*

If for some reason your husband is out of town and you're in charge of your stepchildren, call or email the mother if an issue you're not familiar with comes up. This serves the purpose of keeping her involved and letting her know she is the primary authority over her children, even when she's not there. You'll also build a trusting relationship between the two of you when she sees you actively seeking her opinion on matters relating to her children. In doing that, you demonstrate that you want the best for them as much as she does.

I'm not going to pretend that being a stepmother and building a relationship with the mother of your stepchildren will be easy. There may be instances where you are concerned about the health and safety of your stepchildren, even though they're in their mother's care. What do you do then? As with all things, assess the situation, share your concerns and observations with your husband and act on what feels right to you. Even though you didn't give birth to them, they're your children too.

Building a Relationship with The Ex: Reminders

- *Take it slow.*

- *If she airs concerns about your relationship with her children, discuss them with her - calmly.*

- *Establish the rules for the shared responsibilities of the children.*

- *Be respectful of her feelings - this is an adjustment for her too.*

- *Don't force a friendship that isn't there.*

- *Invite her to family events that include the children. Don't exclude her.*

- *Remember to put the children first.*

CHAPTER SEVEN

Faith and Love:
The Role of Religion in your Relationship

A family that prays together, stays together. But what about the family that doesn't?

Faith is personal, and is the one subject, other than politics, that you probably shouldn't discuss at a dinner party unless you want to be left eating your dessert alone. Religion has a reputation for starting wars and dividing nations going back millennia and continues to stir up uncomfortable questions, which people prefer not to answer.

"So why are you talking about it here, in this book?" you ask. This isn't about getting in your business, telling you how to raise your kids or casting judgment on your spiritual life. When it comes to stepmotherhood, it's about maintaining consistency for the children in your world.

Just as with discipline, bedtime routines, curfews or any other household rule in a blended family, the role and place of faith must also be clear. Is there an expectation that grace will be said before a meal? Would you like your children to attend religious instruction classes? How do you plan to observe holidays specific to your faith? What role will you play in the development of your stepchild's spiritual life? These are straightforward questions, but when they're applied across two households, everyone needs to be on the same page.

The Husband and I were not of one accord where faith was concerned. To this day, I believe it is one of the factors that led to the end of our marriage. Yet the blurred lines that made up my own faith walk as a single woman set the tone for what I brought into our union.

I have always believed in God, yet for many years I failed to live my life in a Christian way. Prayer was infrequent and I rarely opened my Bible. Where my love life was concerned, I didn't comply with any church rules relating to sex. Life changing decisions were made under my own steam and not as the result of a conversation with God. I was out there living my life and not paying any attention to what the Lord I believe in was trying to show me.

When I met my husband, thoughts of faith were distant from both of our minds. He was raised a Muslim, and I, Christian. The way we acted, you never would have thought that our religious beliefs were at one time important to both of us. Yes, we shared our views on faith with each other occasionally, but not in a substantive way. At one time, I asked The Husband how he would like any children we had together to be raised. His answer? "So long as they believe in God, that's okay with me." I was fine with that response, but it should have been a warning. Given that he already had children, the conversation should have been more detailed. How did he envision including me in the children's faith life? What support did he need in explaining things to the children about different religions? How would we mesh the two faiths in our home?

The truth is, if our marriage only featured the two of us, without children in our lives, our lack of cohesion over spiritual matters would have been okay. But as soon as my stepson came to live with us, the cracks started to appear as the absence of a shared vision of faith became evident. Having my stepson with us made me think more about faith, what I was teaching my stepson and what he was learning from us as a household.

More than anything, given the troubled beginnings of Little Man's life, I wanted him to know that there was someone looking over him. I wanted him to know that no matter what life threw his way or how mean people were to him, the God I believed in would always be by his side. Now that I am no longer in Little Man's life, I pray more than ever that he feels that love and is encouraged and comforted by it. Little Man has very few role models in life. Looking up to the Lord isn't a bad place to start.

Spirituality can be good for children for numerous reasons. It can ground them in a set of values they will carry throughout life. It can introduce children to concepts of respect for the law, elders, authority figures, ordinary people and even their pets. A lack of consistency in building up a spiritual dimension to a child's life could leave them short changed in later years.

So how can you begin to approach this? Start with focusing on your own faith values:

- *What aspects of your belief system are important to you?*

- *Do you have a commitment to attending a faith-based service every week?*

- *How comfortable are you talking about religion?*

- *Would you prefer to live in a home where faith wasn't a feature?*

- *If you and your husband practice different faiths, how will this be incorporated into your home life?*

Once you have examined your own faith values and addressed the particular dynamics of spirituality in your own home, consider these steps to creating consistency for your stepchild:

- *Consult with your husband and his ex about the place of faith in their home before the breakup. What are the practices they would like maintained?*

- *Have a conversation with your husband about his views on faith and how he would like it applied in his new home.*

- *If you don't observe certain religious practices, respect that your stepchildren might. For example, if you don't say grace before a meal, but they do, let them.*

- *Encourage open discussion about faith. We have as much to learn from children as they do from us.*

- *On special faith days, try to incorporate all members of the family. This rules out issues of who gets to spend time with the children on significant days.*

- *Stay truthful. Review often, but make sure all of the adults in the relationship maintain an honest, consistent message with the children.*

Everyone has their own take on what faith means to them and even if you are of no faith at all, staying truthful to what works in your home will help your stepchildren as they find their own spiritual path, whether its based in religion or not.

CHAPTER EIGHT

When Two Become One:
Saying Goodbye to the Child That isn't Yours

I'm about to get all Tammy Wynette on you and talk D.I.V.O.R.C.E. Sing it with me, go on, you know you want to. Sadly, it's a song sung all too often in the United States. According to the good people at the Census Bureau, fifty percent of first marriages crash and burn. Think marriages fare better the second time around? Sorry to burst your bubble, but they don't. Divorce rates for those who sign up for "I do, Round Two" is even higher at sixty percent. Put it this way: if a salesman used these figures as part of his pitch for why marriage is a good idea, you'd probably slam the door in his face and run screaming for the hills.

The pain of a breakup is something we've all experienced - whether your high school or college sweetheart or some other brute who you really should have known better than to get involved with. We've all been there.

There is a very specific kind of heartache that comes with a marriage meltdown when you are a stepmother. You're saying goodbye to your present life and your future hopes and dreams. You're also watching the door close on any relationship you have with your stepchild. Now, for some women, not having to deal with a stepchild may bring on the happy dance. If that's you, skip to the next chapter. For those of you who actually like your stepchildren, this is a difficult transition to navigate. Stay with me.

After ten years together, The Husband and I called it quits. The process of removing him from my home was long and drawn out, full of anger and hurt. We started our life together when he moved in with five garbage bags and he returned to his mother's with seven. Give the guy points for progress, right? I wanted him erased from my life, but I was held back by one beautiful little boy. My stepson.

Moving on after a breakup when a child is involved isn't as simple as sliding into a cute outfit, putting on some killer heels and entertaining blind date setups from friends. My heart may have been open to the idea of finding love again some day, but there was nothing that could ever replace Little Man.

That boy was a light in my life. He had my heart from the first moment we met and my love for him only grew deeper and stronger with every year that past. We worked hard to understand one another. As much as he depended on me for help with homework, improving his grades, growing in confidence and building a better life, I depended on him too. He made me a softer person, a kinder person, one not so driven by the demands of corporate America. He made me patient. And he even taught me how to cook better!

Little Man's very presence helped me grow as a person in ways I never imagined. It makes me sad to think that he doesn't even know how much he means to me. At the time of the breakup, I just couldn't fathom a life without him.

Everything fell apart just weeks before Little Man finished the 4th Grade. He was excelling in his studies, had made many friends and was enjoying his life. Breaking the news to him that Daddy and Donna would no longer be together was going to be hard. I wanted to maintain a normal life for him for as long as possible.

Over the years The Husband had witnessed firsthand the love and care I showered on his son. I hadn't carried him for nine months, but I nurtured Little Man as if he was my own flesh. With this in mind, I truly believed The Husband wanted to do all he could to help his son get through this time of transition with the least disruption possible. Yes, I'm that much of an optimist.

We went through the motions of counseling in a half-hearted attempt to save our marriage. It was in vain. The gaping wound between us was so deep that the slightest pressure would burst it wide open again. A Band-Aid wasn't going to fix this. I wasn't interested in healing my marriage. I was fighting for my stepson.

Through all the talking, there was a question suspended in the air like the dampness of a humid day. It was time to clear the sky, so I asked the question The Husband didn't want to hear, "What if Little Man stayed with me, at least until the end of the school year?" After all, it made sense. Consistency for Little Man while The Husband figured out his housing situation and the two of us dealt with the practicalities of the divorce.

As the words left my mouth, the tension in The Husband's body changed the molecular structure of the air around us. The atmosphere was stiff with rage. I, on the other hand, remained as calm as a lake at dawn. My question wasn't crazy; the Husband was heading back to his mother's house, as he had nowhere to live. Plus, he still had two other children to care for. Although my offer was completely about Little Man, it benefited The Husband so much more. He didn't see it that way.

"No, he can't stay with you," he said. "He's my son. You. Are. Not. His. Mother." In that moment, I could have been standing in a boxing ring with Mike Tyson. A punch to the stomach, blows to the head, left and right, a jab to the heart to unsettle my feet, all finished off with a knockout uppercut, rendering me useless on the ground with the referee shouting, "Down for the count!"

Did The Husband really say that? Did he really go *there*? Yes, he did. He was angry and he couldn't handle the fact that I would fight for his son and not for him. But to say those words after all I'd been through with him? I didn't deserve that.

That moment marked the beginning of the end of my relationship with my stepson. After all, The Husband was right. Little Man was not my son. He had a mother and a father and who was I? Sure, I fed him, clothed him and kept a roof over his head when his own parents couldn't. I attended PTA meetings, took an interest in his education, established a routine and gave him a sense of belonging. Yet in the big scheme of things, I was disposable. Easy come, easy go.

There was the inevitable conversation with Little Man about Daddy and Donna not living together any more. The word "divorce" was never used; it's too much for a young child to understand. We told him that things would change, that he would no longer live in the house or go to the same school. Little Man just kept asking, "Why?" I needed him to understand that our decision to "take a break" was in no way his fault.

I'm sure if he'd had a choice, Little Man would have opted to stay with me, if only until the end of the school year, but his loyalty would always be with his first family. In time, he will forget me.

To this day it makes me cry, not spending time with him or knowing how he's doing. I may never know what it's like to bring a child into this world. I will never know, like my own mother, what it's like to lay a child to rest. But I know the void I feel in my heart and I know my relationship with Little Man can never be replaced.

Over time, The Husband collected Little Man's belongings and moved them to his mother's house. I've seen my stepson and his other siblings just a handful of times since then. The emotional impact of the situation is intense and immense and the practical realities are difficult to comprehend. Here are six tips to help you navigate a relationship with your stepchildren after divorce.

TIP ONE: Visitation "rights"' for stepmothers.

The reality is that you don't have any rights, not in the eyes of the law. You can't go to court and fight for custody (if you adopted your stepchildren, this is different and you should speak with an attorney). If the breakup with your ex-husband was amicable, then you may be able to negotiate some time with your stepchildren for special occasions. Remember, you will need the OK from your ex and also his first wife. It's a long chain of command. See how this can get complicated?

TIP TWO: Can you have a relationship with the stepchildren without your ex being involved?

The short answer here is no. On one occasion, my stepchildren asked to meet with me to hang out like we used to. Due to their age, they couldn't travel alone. Their father agreed to drop them off, but I thought he was going to leave and come back to collect them later. No. He decided to stay. Can we say "awkward"? I really had nothing to say to him and the children felt uneasy because they knew we were no longer together.

Having an independent relationship with your stepchildren in this instance is difficult at best. If you can suffer through being in contact with your ex, there's a chance you can make it work. If the two of you can't be within one hundred feet of each other, this may prove a little more of a challenge.

TIP THREE: What happens when you find a new love?

Even if you're still tender from the end of your marriage, one day, you will love again. Honestly, you will. So what happens if you want to visit with you ex's children and your new man doesn't know them? It's a lot to expect your new guy to be involved and there's another consideration too.

A dear friend warned me that it was time to cut ties with my stepchildren once I had a new man in my life. What would happen if the children made accusations of inappropriate behavior by the new guy? Then it would be your word against the children. Who wants to be in that situation? Harsh as it sounds, you must move on and do all you can to protect your new life and your new partner. You don't ever want to think that an adult would put a child up to making such claims, but you just never know. Better to be overly cautious than risk being dragged through the courts.

TIP FOUR: Who do you become? What do the children call you?

This is a tough one. In my case, I was never given a special title, I was only ever Donna. As much as it upset me that I wasn't given a title, if only out of respect, when the marriage came to an end, it was one less piece of the divorce puzzle that had to be removed.

If you *do* have a name your stepchildren call you, think about how this will be handled. If they're young, it may be confusing for them to revert to calling you by your first name.

That said, going from Mommy Donna to Miss Donna, for example, may feel a little too formal. If they are old enough to understand, have the conversation with them. If they're very young, find a way to talk about the breakup and how they would like to address you in terms that will make sense to them.

TIP FIVE: Phone and email contact. Cool or cut?

This very much depends on the age of the child. Of course, you should be able to send a birthday or holiday card without issue - but check with the parents if this could be a problem. Gifts may be awkward, especially if they are high priced items. But phone and email contact? That's personal and not likely to be monitored too closely by your stepchild's parents.

Remember, you want no reason for anyone to accuse you of being inappropriate, so if phone calls, texts and emails are going back and forth, make sure the parents know.

There's another consideration here, especially with texts and emails. You can't be sure that you're actually communicating with your stepchild. Some adults aren't above using their child's phone and email account to go on fact finding missions about their ex. Weird, yes, but not unheard of. Again, as with anything else, use your common sense.

TIP SIX: Protecting a child's feelings

One of the most heartbreaking text messages I ever received was from my stepdaughter. Because we were no longer in touch, she thought that I hated her and her siblings. That couldn't be further from the truth. I loved those children, but The Husband made it difficult for us to be in contact. Could I have done more to protect their feelings? Yes, but this would have meant going head to head with my ex husband and the children's mother, and I just couldn't do that.

There's no easy way to navigate this element of your marriage breakdown. There's no way to guard your heart. I can't tell you that you won't feel hurt, confused and disappointed. And even though The Husband said many untrue things in our marriage, he spoke one very clear truth when he said I was not the mother of his children. There's no way to change that.

These days, I catch snippets of my stepchildren's lives here and there and remain grateful for the small part I played in their upbringing. I'd love to do more, but that's as far as my rights go. Today, my life continues, all the better for knowing my stepchildren.

CHAPTER NINE

You, Me and Baby Makes Three:
Motherhood vs. Stepmotherhood

First comes love, then comes marriage, then comes baby in a baby carriage. Oh, the innocence of children's playground songs and the simplicity of their world view. If only life was so straightforward!

Deciding when and if to have a child can be a complicated process with many things to consider: finances, space, childcare, maternity leave, paternity leave and the impact a little person will have on your life and your relationship.

Imagine this: You're married. Your husband has children from a previous relationship. They're no longer babies and his nights of diaper changes through puffy, sleep-deprived eyes are long gone. He doesn't have to worry about any kind of baby-produced fluid running down his crisp work shirt. He's done his bit for the continuation of the human race and is looking forward to the days when his little ones are grown, independent and out of his home.

You, on the other hand, have yet to embrace the joys of parenthood, but you're ready to sign on the dotted line. You love your stepchildren, but you want a child of your own, a symbol of the love you and your husband share. The trouble is, the love of your life has made it clear that he's not interested in creating another Mini-Me. At all. So what do you do if you want a child, but in your husband's mind, his family is already complete?

The child conversation is one that needs to be had early and often. How early? Ok, maybe not on a first date. But when it's clear that the two of you are doing more than dinner and a movie every now and then, open your mouth and get the ball rolling. Talking about family-building after you're married is too late, especially if *not* having a child is a deal breaker for you. It's harsh, but better to know now rather than later. Yes, life is about compromise and nowhere is this more evident than in relationships. But are you willing to walk away from the chance of being a mother to your own child simply because the man you fell in love with already has kids? Be honest with yourself and your feelings, because once the biological clock runs out, it's hard to find a way back.

There is, of course, another scenario. What if your husband, who is already a father, wants more children, but you don't? That's the situation I was in. In my Twenties, I desperately wanted to start a family and be a mother, but there was never the right time or the right guy. In theory, once married, I'd met "Mr Right" and there was no reason to hold back. So why did the idea of having kids with The Husband feel so wrong?

Let's examine the evidence. It was clear that The Husband loved his children, he demonstrated this over and over again. Any time he was with them, they laughed, smiled broadly and enjoyed his company.

My concern lay firmly in his inability to care and provide for them on a practical level. Kids need love, no question, but they also need clothes, shoes, food, medical attention and dental care. The Husband was unable to provide any of that, and nor did he try. Put plainly, I wasn't confident that - God forbid something happened to me - he could step up and raise our child the right way, as an engaged, responsible and solvent parent.

Of course, I couldn't share my misgivings with him. The Husband is one of eighteen - yes, I said eighteen - so fathering any number of children still in the single digits wasn't an issue for him. For most people, the thought of more than a car-full of kids is enough to hit the brakes.

However, peer pressure accounts for a lot. Even though I was secretly okay with the idea of not having a child with The Husband, once I was married, everyone seemed to have an opinion on the activities of my womb. Comments like "So when's the baby coming?" or, "You're not getting any younger. Don't leave it too long!" Everyone from the mailman to the woman at the hair salon thought it was perfectly acceptable to comment on my ovary action. Forget about the annual State of the Union address. It was a daily State of the Uterus.

The pressure to conceive also came from an unusual source - The Husband's Ex. More than anyone, she really had no place in my reproductive organs, yet she walked right in. Let me explain. After she threw Little Man out, The Husband went to court for custody of his boy. The whole case threw her into a rage and the target of her anger was me, even though I wasn't in the courtroom. According to The Husband, his ex said:

"You're only fighting for custody of my son because *she* can't have kids."

I'd be lying if I said her words didn't hurt. Who wants to think of their womb, the hub of all new life, as a broken machine, unfit for use? And more to the point, who told her we were having problems conceiving? I don't know if The Husband told her. If he did, why did he see fit to discuss our business with his baby-mama? And if he didn't, why, oh why did he think I would want to hear such a thing? From her? What hurt the most, is that The Husband didn't protect me.

By repeating the Ex's cruel words, he'd left me vulnerable in the most intimate of ways. Never one to let others get the upper hand, I decided it was time to make a baby, if only to prove her wrong.

Embarking on the road to motherhood should be simple. Boy meets girl. Girl likes boy. Boy and girl show each other how much they like each other. Girl gets pregnant. Lots of smiling faces. Baby arrives. We all live happily ever after. The End.

Back in the real world that is my life, Operation Baby was a journey filled with potholes and ditches. Attempts to get pregnant as nature intended produced nothing other than disappointment. So we put our hopes - along with our best genetic matter - into the hands of a fertility doctor.

Walking into the first round of IVF, we had hope. Friends who had also struggled trying to conceive hit the jackpot with their first in vitro fertilization procedure. I was certain the same would happen for us. So I gladly took every drug, every painful shot, every invasive doctor's appointment, because at the end we'd have a baby.

That's not what happened. IVF 1. Donna and The Husband 0.

I was stunned. The Husband was shocked and disappointed. It was only then that I realized just how much he wanted to extend his family. For this reason, we decided to jump back into the ring.

This time, we knew what to expect. Needless to say I wasn't as gleeful when it came to taking the drugs and administering the shots. The stakes were high before, but now it felt as though we were climbing Mount Everest. The doctor harvested more eggs, The Husband donated more sperm. We prayed for a miracle and...nothing. IVF 2. Donna and The Husband 0.

How much pain can a person take? I was bitter and angry that my body wouldn't cooperate and just hold on to the life that was being created. The pressure mounted, as Little Man continued to ask for a little brother to play with and The Husband looked on, crushed by yet another negative pregnancy test.

In the midst of the anxiety I was thankful for a good medical insurance policy which covered the vast majority of the costs. I was able to pay the remainder, but The Husband contributed not one dime. Why? Because he couldn't afford it. Nor did he try. The story of our marriage.

Between carrying the financial load of our household and bearing the pain of the IVF treatment, I really questioned the wisdom of trying to have a baby with The Husband. If I'm honest, I'd had doubts even before we started the journey.

Let's look at the facts. He didn't have a steady income. He was behind on child support for his two children who lived with their mother. He relied on me for almost everything. Was this really the best environment to raise a child in?

Somewhere, I put all of these thoughts to the back of my mind and we went ahead with two more rounds of IVF. Round three was a bust. Round four, I produced twenty great eggs! My faith was restored, after all, you only need one!

Even with the increased odds of success, I felt beyond ill. The drugs, the stress, the financial burden - everything - put me in the emergency room.

My blood pressure was off the charts and I knew I could never go through this again. I had nothing more to give and I couldn't rely on The Husband to replenish me.

Not one of those twenty eggs fertilized. Four years of treatment and thousands of dollars in medical bills later, we had what we'd started the journey with: nothing. Okay, you win. I'm taking my eggs and going home. IVF 4. Donna and The Husband 0.

The experience left me broken and feeling less of a woman. It was no longer about proving a point to The Ex. I didn't care about her and the rancid words that fell from her mouth in the courtroom. I just couldn't get over the loss of all of that potential life. All those eggs and not *one* made it. Yet, I knew in my heart that we hadn't conceived for a reason. If we had, I would be forever tied to The Husband. Did I really want that?

As I grieved the children we would never have, the pieces of the puzzle that would mark the end of our marriage were yet to fall into place, but something within me knew we wouldn't stay together. Every vision I had of life with our child revolved around me raising the little one alone. The Husband was never in the picture. I had witnessed firsthand his failure to provide for his children, why would he be any different with ours? A sad admission, but the truth.

Children are a blessing and a miracle, even in the most straightforward cases. They flip your world upside down, make you question everything you do and force you to view your life through a different lens. You have to be ready - as an individual and as a unit.

In putting this book together, I've heard countless stories about the strain a child can put on a blended family. If your husband has children and doesn't want more, ask why. If he's a good man and cares about the people he's bringing into the world, it may be hard for him to fathom raising more children. He may worry about the additional financial responsibility, the increasing demands on his time and the curtailing of what little freedom he has left. Your husband's worries are valid and not a reflection on how much he loves you and values your relationship.

The very fact that he's thinking through such a life-changing decision speaks volumes about just how much he cares about you and your family.

But before you get into full on baby-making mode, here are some things to consider:

- *What if the situation isn't right?*

Men want children too. In my case, it was The Husband who

wanted to increase his tribe. Just because you can, doesn't mean to say you should have kids. If your beau's not taking care of the little ones he already has, or it's clear he can't afford to have anymore, have the conversation. If he still doesn't understand why having another child isn't a great idea, then you have a decision to make .

- *Respect how you feel*

What if your husband decides that he really can't face having any more children? Seek help, get counseling and talk it through. If you've always wanted to be a mother to your own child but your husband says no, don't sweep that feeling under the rug. Your marriage may not survive.

- *Respect how he feels*

The basis of marriage is honesty and if your husband says no to more children, even though you may not like it, you must respect it. If he feels forced into having another child, this could backfire years down the line. If this is a deal breaker, again, you have a tough decision to make.

- *What do you do if you both want a child and nothing is happening?*

Undergoing fertility treatment is hard physically, mentally and emotionally. If for some reason you can't get pregnant, prepare for unsolicited remarks from friends and random people such as "Well, at least you have stepchildren, so there will always be kids around," or "He has kids, why would you want more?" Well-meaning, certainly, but so annoying. Discuss all of the options with your husband and deal with people however you see fit. If that means cutting some folks off for a while, then do it. There is life after infertility, whether that's adoption, IVF or living child-free.

- *Decide who you're going to share your family building plans with.*

Trying to conceive is stressful. Well-meaning family members may add to that pressure by asking if you're pregnant yet and if you're not, why is it taking so long? Even if you love your family, they don't need to be involved in all aspects of your life. It's okay to keep people out of your womb.

- *When you get pregnant, decide who to tell first.*

This is a delicate job. While you will want your stepchildren to be among the first to know, it's guaranteed they will share the news with their mother. If you or your husband have a good relationship with his ex- wife, it would be a nice gesture to tell her in person, rather than have her discover the news via the children.

- *Involve the children.*

If you're already a stepmother to young children, involve them in the baby's life from as early as you feel comfortable. Remember, having to explain a miscarriage will hurt more than keeping the children in the dark for a little while. Adding another child to the mix can be unsettling for young children and raise concerns about how much Daddy loves them, how important they will be once the new baby arrives and if they will still get all the special treats they're used to. Include the soon-to-be older siblings in shopping trips for the baby, ask their opinion on names and make them feel even more loved than they already are.

Whatever happens, everything is for a reason. The Husband and I never had a child together and it became clear why at the end of our marriage. "Donna," he said, "I cheated on you because you can't have kids." Stunned, betrayed and broken, I knew as the words hit me one by one, that the pain of the four failed IVF treatments had saved me from a lifetime of contact with a man who neither loved nor respected me.

Be at peace with whatever decision you make. Not having a child may be the best thing that ever happens to you.

CHAPTER TEN

Neither Wife nor Mother:
Negotiating the Role of Stepgirlfriend

When in doubt about the meaning of a word, you can always trust Merriam-Webster to provide a definition. So here's one:

> **girlfriend** -- *noun* \ˈgər(-ə)l-ˌfrend\
>
> 1: a female friend
>
> 2: a frequent or regular female companion in a romantic or sexual relationship

Here's another.

> **stepmother** -- *noun* \-ˌmə-<u>th</u>ər\ : the wife of one's father when distinct from one's natural or legal mother

OK. So what about the woman who is a frequent female companion of one's father who is distinct from one's natural or legal mother? Huh? Merriam-Webster what've you got? Oh, that would be *nothing*.

You see, there is no definition for a woman who is romantically linked, but not married to, a man with children. She's more than a friend, but she's not the wife nor is she the stepmother. There's no official name for her. So we will call her the Stepgirlfriend.

Society no longer frowns upon divorce or sex outside of

marriage, so newly single men are in no rush to find a replacement bride to keep up appearances. This leaves the way open for a woman on the dating scene to find herself in the Stepgirlfriend Zone. Don't fret. It's not a crazy place where strange things happen, but the potential for confusion is high in that space between dating and wife.

In this realm, there are so many questions to be asked. When should the stepgirlfriend be introduced to the children? What role will she play in their lives? What are the emotional dangers of stepchildren and stepgirlfriends building a strong relationship? What discipline rights does the stepgirlfriend have? What are the rules of engagement when it comes to the stepgirlfriend and the ex-wife? If marriage is in the cards, is another child part of the plan too? And what pressure could this put on the family unit?

Wait, what was that sound? Oh yes, that was your chin hitting the floor. A lot to digest, isn't it? The truth is, navigating the world as a stepmother is difficult enough, but the challenges increase exponentially as a stepgirlfriend. Your position lacks permanence, you'll most certainly be seen as a threat to the status quo and you not only have to impress your new beau, you'll also have to win over the hearts and minds of his children. Did I also mention his ex? Frankly, it's enough to make you want to lie down in a darkened room with an ice-cold compress surgically attached to your forehead. Failing that, knowing you're not alone can help.

During our dating days, The Husband's children were not a day-to-day fixture and I played just a small role in their lives. Little was expected of me in a mother capacity and I didn't feel a need to insert my opinion into how The Husband and his ex were raising their children. I cared, but I was an outsider.

While my experience as a married stepmother has armed me with practical tools to help anyone taking on a new husband and his brood, I have little to offer by way of personal testimony to all the stepgirlfriend mamas. I didn't want to leave you out, so I turned to one woman who is neither a wife nor a natural born mother.

For the last two years Brenda has supported her boyfriend through a messy, ongoing divorce. Through it all, she's come to learn more than she ever thought possible about love, children and new definitions of family.

Here's her story:

My life is complicated. High octane, time-crunched, wonderful and rewarding, but complicated. Two years ago, life was simple. Me then: a career woman who loved her work, her clients, the buzz of success and a job well done. The word "failure" didn't exist. Away from the office, I had time to be a good friend, sister, daughter and aunt while indulging in life's pleasures: good food, good wine, good music and beautiful shoes.

My life wasn't perfect. There were things that I wanted, but for the most part, everything was handled. I was answerable to no-one and could do as I pleased. If I wanted to stay late at the office, I could. There was no one waiting to greet me with a dirty look or a disapproving, "What time do you call this?" tap on the watch.

So what changed? I met a great guy. I wasn't looking for a

family. I wasn't looking to have my world turned upside down. I was just out having fun on a date, trying to regain some balance. What I got caught me off guard. What I got was Derrick. A funny, handsome, super smart, warm hearted, computer nerd who happened to have two kids.

For some people, the word "children" would have them downing their drink at the table and running out the door with their jacket half on. But I had no issue with Derrick's children. Sitting there on our first date, they weren't my concern and as far as I knew never would be. Neither of us had mentioned a second date, so why should I clog my head with a scenario that may never play out?

However, there was a second date and many after that. I learned more about Derrick's life, including the messy separation from his wife, his new life as a part-time single dad and the importance of his children. It was clear from the outset that if we were to be together, I had to be a part of the unit. Becoming part of Derrick's family came with its own problems, challenges and moments of frustration. But what I gained can't be quantified.

There are no set rules for being a stepgirlfriend - there are as many different scenarios for this family dynamic as there are people on the planet. What I *can* offer are my own insights and observations on the curveballs I was thrown and how I coped: catching some, dodging others and getting smacked in the face by many. Here are my top four to look out for:

- *My Life vs. Family Life*

- *Emotional vulnerability*

- *The difficulties of discipline*

- *Finding my place in a new family*

My Life vs. Family Life

Mother nature does a wonderful thing with pregnancy - she gives everyone involved nine months to get their head around the fact that life is about to change in a major way. Not so for stepmothers and stepgirlfriends. It was like I clicked my heels three times and went from single woman to mother and de facto wife in an instant. I was certainly not in Kansas anymore.

When I went out on my first date with Derrick, I wasn't looking for a family. If I was actively seeking the trappings of marriage, the adjustment from my life of me to a life of family would have been much easier. For the first time ever in my personal life, I had to compromise and it was hard.

A new relationship has needs. Children have even more. For Derrick, putting his children first came without a second thought, especially in the toxic fallout of the breakup from his wife. He wanted to recreate an environment of familial warmth and I was a part of that. He was clear the children had a mother and I wasn't to replace her, but I had a role in their lives - something along the lines of a favored aunt.

I was overwhelmed. There was my big job, big mortgage, instant big family, full time boyfriend and another home to manage. Somewhere in there I still wanted my life: late nights at the office, time to pursue my hobbies and evenings with friends. All of the above was a no-no. Late home for dinner? Derrick accused me of not prioritizing the family. Off for a night out with friends? The oldest child would make puppydog eyes and ask, "Why are you leaving us? Again?" Feel guilty much?

The toughest transition had nothing to do with the children. It was all down to my phone. "Why don't you call to let me know where you are?" said Derrick. Yes, I was expected to "check in." I had never "checked in" with anyone! Why would I? I was an autonomous being! The simple act of making a call to say I was heading home, or popping into the store or grabbing a drink with a colleague filled me with resentment. I felt trapped by this family, even though I loved them and wanted to be a part of their world.

Over time, compromise has become easier - I want to be home for dinner and spend time with my family. It continues to be a battle to find a balance between the needs of the children and our needs as a couple. In order to be a part of family mealtime, I have to leave work before all of my tasks are complete. This then means playing catch up once the children return to their mom, which in turn means the time Derrick and I spend together alone as a couple is cut short. Carving out that time to stay connected is tough - but then, isn't it the same for every couple with children?

Emotional Vulnerability

Derrick's children were just one and seven when I met them, briefly, for the first time. Just two months into our relationship, I was a regular feature in their lives. Of course, it was way too soon. Derrick was still coming to terms with being a single father, the children were adjusting to their new reality and there I was another adult to think about.

It was a vulnerable time for everyone involved, but especially the children. They loved their dad, that was clear, but when they were with him in their "other" home, they craved female attention. I was able to fill that role in the moment, but in hindsight, the children were in emotional danger from such a quick, deep attachment. What if I decided to walk away? What if Derrick called "time" on us? My very presence and bond with the children had set them up for additional pain in their lives. For months, the thought of doing anything that hurt them kept me awake at night.

Emotional vulnerability is a two-way street. While the children became attached to me, I became attached to them, the younger child especially. At just one year old, the baby accepted me with no questions asked. While Derrick tended to his older child and his issues around the separation, I spent hours one-on-one with the baby. In many ways, that little one feels like a piece of me. I can't begin to think of life without either of them, but as a stepgirlfriend, there's always a question mark over your place.

That question mark fuels fear. Fear of inadequacy. Fear that my inadequacy will lead to losing Derrick. Fear of rejection. Fear that one day I will want out. Fear that my actions will harm or damage the children in some way. I'm no stranger to children in my life, but steering kids through an unfamiliar family dynamic - and an incendiary one at that - was new. So I found myself in the local library reading child development books - because I have a stack of free time on my hands, right? But I wanted to do better, to be better for the children. And I wanted to stop fearing failure.

This fear never goes away. Children have a way of making you feel bad for nothing. Some days I don't know what kind of reception I will get from the older child. Will I get a wide smile and a hug? Or will the door be slammed firmly in my face? Most of the time, the mean words and actions roll off my back. These are kids in transition and I understand there's alot of confusion around them, but I'm human and some days it just hurts. I can't hold back though. Emotionally, I can't live as though I won't be with them in two months, six months or a year. When you're a stepgirlfriend, you have to love, keep loving and love a little bit more, even when you don't want to.

The Difficulties of Discipline

What's the quickest way to start a fight among ordinarily amenable mamas and papas? Start talking about discipline. Everyone has views on how to keep children in line - from time-outs and incentives to an old-school whopping. But even though discipline is a cornerstone of child rearing, Derrick and I never discussed it.

We weren't officially co-parenting, so in many ways a conversation wasn't necessary. We'd established my role as an aunt-type figure - one with a level of authority but with no disciplinary power.

This was fine until my responsibilities within our informal family grew. Derrick would call on me to watch the kids solo and of course on occasion they would act up. Was I supposed to *not* discipline them in his absence and turn a blind eye? I was no longer a guest in the home and had closely observed Derrick's discipline style, so I stepped in and handled any poor behavior in the moment.

Right there, I'd created unintended conflict. I don't live my life monitoring all of my actions, so after a while, if we were out as a family and one of the children did something they shouldn't, I would step in and chastise them without a second thought. Derrick was not okay with this development. He saw me disciplining his child while he was not part of the process and he got scared. Me exercising authority over his child wasn't the problem. We'd just never talked about it, so we had no framework for such situations.

What amused me though, was how I really wasn't given any instructions for caring for Derrick's children alone. On the other hand, the first time my sister babysat them she was given a laundry list of contact names and numbers along with army precision instructions on how to look after the kids. I wish I'd been prepped in the same way.

Finding my place in the Family

The word "family" was both emotionally charged and unspoken in our house. From early on, I claimed Derrick and his children as my own, but the word really was a landmine. Derrick's older child was clear he already had a family, which did *not* include me.

I was never trying to be the children's mother, I could never take that job. In the early days, trying to do "family stuff" was hard - in many ways I was sitting in the mother's seat. Even every day moments like family dinner were difficult.

I expected the children to take a moment to adjust to the expanded version of their family, but Derrick's reaction shocked me. It's hard to be close to children - even if they are not your blood children - to love them and care for them and interact with them as if they're your own and not view them as your kids. Not seeing them as mine only created a distance that in my heart just wasn't there.

Derrick had a problem with me "claiming" his children. "Do you know their teachers' names?" he asked. " No," I replied. "Then you have not earned the right to the title. You can't claim them as yours." To this day, those words hurt. It's unclear what I call them, but they are mine. If I walked this journey as if they were simply my boyfriend's kids, we would all be poorer for it. I know I didn't give birth to them, but I know who those children are to me, and they know how special they are. And that's all that matters.

The longer we spend together, the nature of our family unit and the relationships within it deepen. The children tell me they love me. The older child no longer fears talking about their mother in my presence. Even my cooking has won praise! But the moment I knew this was all worthwhile was when I was invited to take a "family photo" on the couch. No drama, no angst, just an invitation to commit to a picture our imperfect but beautiful family.

There are no easy answers to how to cope with being a

stepgirlfriend. Derrick and I continue to argue as we try to find our way through the maze of parenthood, his messy divorce and the well-being of his children. Just as we attain a level of peace in one place, there's another fire to put out elsewhere.

Trying to control the process is pointless - there are too many variables you have no say in - such as his ex-wife. No matter what, if your boyfriend has children, she will always be in your lives. Respect the fact and move on. Annoying as it can be, it's easier.

If you can, try to casually preempt any issues that may arise. A friendly conversation over breakfast or during a walk in the park. Some key conversations that Derrick and I missed include the rules of disciplining the children, your place in the family and expectations surrounding your time as a family. And be all in. Loving from a distance is no good for you, the children or your relationship.

People ask me, if I could go back and do this again, would I choose to be with a man with children? I can't answer that. All I know is that this is the life I live today and I wouldn't change a thing.

I'm a better person for the tough times we've endured and my life has more balance and meaning that it has in years. Yes, there are challenges, but there are great rewards and that's what I focus on every day with my little family.

CHAPTER ELEVEN

All's Well That Ends Well:
Life After Stepmotherhood

January 2013. I'm sitting in a café chatting with a friend and deciding whether I should forget my diet and have fries with my lunch when my phone beeps. A decade of my life is brought to a close with an email. My divorce is final.

Even though The Husband had been out of my life and physical space for over a year, that last piece of legal business meant I was officially free. Not that I needed permission to get on with my life, but there was no chance of this chapter coming back from the dead. Well, that's not strictly true. There were the bills The Husband left me with and the rest of the financial fallout which I'll be dealing with for a while, but you get my point.

I miss the children. I miss their chatter and laughter. I miss their questioning and their company. I think about Little Man everyday. I pray he's doing ok. In my heart I will always be a stepmother. Those children are a part of me and I will carry them wherever I go, even though we no longer see each other or communicate. Who knows, maybe as adults we can be friends, but for now, I know that door is closed.

Life goes on and how quickly things change. It's August 2013, and, as I write this, I think of how different my life was ten years ago, five years ago, two years ago, a year ago. The Donna Jarrett of today is very different from her previous incarnations. Would I change even one thing about my marriage and life as a stepmother? No. Every experience has brought me to this place where I can share my story and I hope that it will help you too. Through my mistakes and missteps, may you find the courage to make better choices for yourself and your future happiness.

Today, I sit here a stronger woman, full of hope and excitement for the future. And I sit here full of love with my best friend and new husband. Yes, I remarried. No, he doesn't have kids. He was the one for me all along. It just took me over twenty years and a few twists, turns, detours and a marriage to realize it.

Real life is not a fairytale and being a stepmother is no walk in the park, but every story deserves a happy ending.

Go and find yours.

You'll find more resources, articles and details on events relating to being a stepmother at ItTakesAVillageToday.com

– I'm with you every step of the way.

ABOUT THE AUTHOR

Growing up in the Bronx, Donna Jarrett witnessed firsthand the sacrifices needed to raise a family, thanks to her hard working parents. Their dedication to their children lay the foundation for Donna's future career as a hard working Executive for the last two decades.

In 2008, Donna's entrepreneurial spirit led to the creation of "It Takes A Village Today," an online marketing company. As founder and CEO, Jarrett offers exposure to small businesses which struggle to be heard in the crowded media landscape.

Donna's relentless drive to pursue excellence has made her a sought after speaker for youth and business leaders alike. She's the proud recipient of the Heroes of Humanity award from the Rockland County Commission on Human Rights. With a passion for the arts, Donna produced a highly acclaimed Off-Broadway show which ran for two months. Her involvement in the budgeting, talent bookings and auditions is what gave "It Takes A Village Today," the zeal to pursue other areas of business.

Donna now adds author to her extensive list of accomplishments. *"You're Not My Mommy!" WARNINGS from an Ex-Stepmother"* recounts her very modern experience of love, marriage and living in a very modern family dynamic.

Donna currently resides in New York and is newly married.

"You're Not My Mommy!" WARNINGS from an Ex-Stepmother

www.ingramcontent.com/pod-product-compliance
Lightning Source LLC
Chambersburg PA
CBHW071140090426
42736CB00012B/2182